P9-CCD-900

The
Russian
Americans

The
Russian
Americans

Other books in the
Immigrants in America series:

The Chinese Americans
The Cuban Americans
The Italian Americans
The Vietnamese Americans

The
Russian
Americans

By Meg Greene Malvasi

LUCENT BOOKS
SAN DIEGO, CALIFORNIA

THOMSON
★
™
GALE

Detroit • New York • San Diego • San Francisco
Boston • New Haven, Conn. • Waterville, Maine
London • Munich

Library of Congress Cataloging-in-Publication Data

Greene Malvasi, Meg.
   The Russian Americans / by Meg Greene Malvasi.
       p. cm. — (Immigrants in America)
Includes bibliographical references and index.
Summary: Discusses the diverse ethnicity of Russian Americans, their
immigration, Jewish community, social, cultural and political customs,
employment, experiences with discrimination, and integration into
American society.
   ISBN 1-56006-963-5 (alk. paper)
1. Russian Americans—History—Juvenile literature. 2. Russian
Americans—Social conditions—Juvenile literature. 3. Immigrants—
United States—History—Juvenile literature. 4. Russia—Emigration
and immigration—History—Juvenile lierature. 5. United States—
Emigration and immigration—History—Juvenile literature.
[1. Russian Americans. 2. Russia—Emigration and immigration—
History. 3. United States—Emigration and immigration—History.]
I.Title. II. Series.
   E184.R9 G74 2002
   973'.049171—dc21

                                          2001003959

Copyright © 2002 by Lucent Books,
an imprint of The Gale Group
10911 Technology Place, San Diego, CA 92127

No part of this book may be reproduced or used in any form or by
any means, electrical, mechanical, or otherwise, including, but not
limited to, photocopy, recording, or any information storage and
retrieval system, without prior written permission from the publisher.

Printed in the USA

CONTENTS

FOREWORD

Immigrants have come to America at different times, for different reasons, and from many different places. They leave their homelands to escape religious and political persecution, poverty, war, famine, and countless other hardships. The journey is rarely easy. Sometimes, it entails a long and hazardous ocean voyage. Other times, it follows a circuitous route through refugee camps and foreign countries. At the turn of the twentieth century, for instance, Italian peasants, fleeing poverty, boarded steamships bound for New York, Boston, and other eastern seaports. And during the 1970s and 1980s, Vietnamese men, women, and children, victims of a devastating war, began arriving at refugee camps in Arkansas, Pennsylvania, Florida, and California, en route to establishing new lives in the United States.

Whatever the circumstances surrounding their departure, the immigrants' journey is always made more difficult by the knowledge that they leave behind family, friends, and a familiar way of life. Despite this, immigrants continue to come to America because, for many, the United States represents something they could not find at home: freedom and opportunity for themselves and their children.

No matter what their reasons for emigrating, where they have come from, or when they left, once here, nearly all immigrants face considerable challenges in adapting and making the United States

their new home. Language barriers, unfamiliar surroundings, and sometimes hostile neighbors make it difficult for immigrants to assimilate into American society. Some Vietnamese, for instance, could not read or write in their native tongue when they arrived in the United States. This heightened their struggle to communicate with employers who demanded they be literate in English, a language vastly different from their own. Likewise, Irish immigrant school children in Boston faced classmates who teased and belittled their lilting accent. Immigrants from Russia often felt isolated, having settled in areas of the United States where they had no access to traditional Russian foods. Similarly, Italian families, used to certain wines and spices, rarely shopped or traveled outside of New York's Little Italy, a self-contained community cut off from the rest of the city.

Even when first-generation immigrants do successfully settle into life in the United States, their children, born in America, often have different values and are influenced more by their country of birth than their parents' traditions. Children want to be a part of the American culture and usually welcome American ideals, beliefs, and styles. As they become more Americanized—adopting western dating habits and fashions, for instance—they tend to cast aside or even actively reject the traditions embraced by their parents. Assimilation, then, often becomes an ideological dispute that creates conflict among immigrants of every ethnicity. Whether Chinese, Italian, Russian, or Vietnamese, young people battle their elders for respect, individuality, and freedom, issues that often would not have come up in their homeland. And no matter how tightly the first generations hold onto their traditions, in the end, it is usually the young people who decide what to keep and what to discard.

The Immigrants in America series fully examines the immigrant experience. Each book in the series discusses why the immigrants left their homeland, what the journey to America was like, what they experienced when they arrived, and the challenges of assimilation. Each volume includes discussion of triumph and tragedy, contributions and influences, history and the future. Fully documented primary and secondary source quotations enliven the text. Sidebars highlight interesting events and personalities. Annotated bibliographies offer ideas for additional research. Each book in this dynamic series provides students with a wealth of information as well as launching points for further discussion.

INTRODUCTION

Russians in America

According to government statistics, approximately 6.5 million people from all over the world immigrated to the United States between 1990 and 1998. Of these new arrivals, almost 400,000 came from Russia, joining an already sizable Russian American population that numbers more than 1 million persons today.

Although not the largest group to come to the United States, the Russians have maintained an important presence in America for more than two hundred years. Like their country, the Russian immigrants are an intriguing and diverse group that brought with them to the United States a rich culture, history, and tradition.

An Early Presence

The early history of exploration and settlement in North America is a history dominated by the Spanish, Dutch, French, and English. However, the Russians, too, were important in settling the continent, especially the regions that became Alaska, western Canada, and the northwestern United States.

The first Russian explorers in North America came not to establish new settlements but to find new sources of animal furs. By 1763, the year in which the English established their supremacy over most of eastern North America, the Russians had been present in the Aleutian Islands off the coast of Alaska for almost twenty years. During that time they had explored most of Kodiak Island, located at the easternmost tip of the Aleutians, where, in 1784, they established the first permanent Russian settlement in North America.

The Russians were encouraged enough by the initial success of their Alaska venture to push for expansion, this time south toward California. In 1812, they established Fort Ross, a fur-trading outpost located just north of San Francisco. But as a commercial venture, the California colony was a failure, due to the inhabitants' inability to sustain the fort's operations. Traders depleted the otter population and were unable to make the move from hunting to farming, a change that might have bolstered the settlement. Thus, in 1842, the Russians abandoned California and sold the fort to American merchant John Sutter.

A Special Relationship

Perhaps because of their long history on the continent, the Russians have held a special fascination for the American people. During the twentieth century, the histories of the two countries were closely intertwined, and relations between them not always cordial. Like immigrants from other lands, the Russians came to the United States at first to find better opportunities and the chance to start a new life. By the twentieth century, however, many were fleeing Russia to escape communism, an oppressive and brutal governmental system that put many Russians in fear for their lives.

Today, the number of Russians coming to the United States continues to grow at a steady pace. Close to half of them live in the northeast region of the United States, establishing close-knit communities in cities such as New York and Boston. A large number of Russian immigrants have also settled in the mid-Atlantic states of New Jersey and Pennsylvania. Approximately one-third reside in the west and northwest regions of the United States, including the states of California and Washington. Fewer have gravitated to the Midwest, settling in cities like Chicago, and the South, to states such as Florida and Texas. Many have become American citizens, but they have not abandoned their past, their culture, or their faith.

Some Special Challenges

Even though Russians have become a fixed part of American society, the history of the Russian immigrant experience is often difficult to study because in many ways the Russians remained isolated from mainstream American life. They spoke a bewildering language and believed in a religion that was vastly different from other Christian faiths. Furthermore, many of the nineteenth and twentieth-century immigrants aligned themselves with unpopular political causes that, to many Americans, seemed to pose a real threat to U.S. standards, values, and ideals. All of these factors helped dissociate Russians from Americans, and dissuaded the immigrants from more fully assimilating to their new country.

Closely intertwined with these problems were those of national and cultural identity. By the outbreak of World War I in 1914,

Immigrants await medical examinations at the Immigration building on New York's Ellis Island.

approximately 1 million immigrants had arrived from the Russian empire to settle in the United States. The majority of these early arrivals, however, were not Russian at all. They were, instead, the descendants of the German Russians whom Catherine the Great had invited to settle in Russia during the late eighteenth century, or they were peoples whose homelands the Russians had conquered and incorporated into their empire, such as the Ukrainians, Latvians, Lithuanians, Estonians, and Poles. By far, though, the majority of Russian immigrants who came to the United States were Jew-

ish. Being Jewish in Russia has always involved special challenges and hardships, the least difficult of which was maintaining their distinct cultural and religious traditions.

A Diverse People

Russian Americans also came from a variety of backgrounds, from peasants and factory workers to writers, artists, musicians, doctors, and lawyers. Some of the most recent arrivals are those from middle- and upper-class backgrounds who worked as government administrators in the former Soviet Union. Russian athletes have also made America their home. During the last decade, the sport of hockey has enjoyed a renewed vigor and energy in the United States, thanks in part to the many Russian hockey players from the Red Army and other Soviet hockey teams who have come to the United States to play professionally for American teams.

Some of Russia's greatest losses have been America's gain, as a number of gifted Russian artists, scientists, and scholars have come to the United States. Among some of the more well known of these émigrés are dancers and choreographers George Bal-anchine, Natalia Makarova, and Mikhail Baryshnikov, and writers and poets Joseph Brodsky, Vladimir Nabokov, and Irina Raushinskaya. Russian immigrant Louise Nevelson broke new ground in the American art scene with her environmental sculptures, and Vladimir Horowitz, considered one of the great piano virtuosos of the twentieth century called America home for most of his life, having left the Soviet Union in 1925.

The United States has also benefited in innumerable ways from the scientific and technical knowledge of Russian immigrants. The field of American aviation might not have advanced so far or so fast

The United States has benefited immensely from the contributions of Russian immigrants, including Igor Sikorsky (far right), inventor of the helicopter.

without the contributions of Igor Sikorsky, the inventor of the helicopter. Other Russian scientists have made important discoveries in the fields of physics and chemistry. In addition, Russian scholars have helped Americans better understand the history of Russia; the field of Russian studies in colleges and universities continues to expand as a new generation of scholars arrives in the United States to teach and write.

Today, it is relatively easy for people wishing to leave Russia to do so, although it was not always that way. Czars and Soviet leaders were, adamant that Russians not emigrate, and often, American government officials restricted immigration with laws that limited the number of people who could move to the United States. However, with the easing of immigration restrictions during the late 1970s and the collapse of the Soviet Union in 1991, there remain virtually no legal restrictions for those who wish to leave Russia and come to the United States.

Changing Attitudes

Investigating the ways in which Russian immigrants adjusted to their new lives in the United States is in some respects a testament to how well the American system of government and way of life works. The majority of Russian immigrants came from a country that was in direct political opposition to the United States; in fact, many Russians were brought up to believe that America was their country's greatest enemy. Yet many came, and continue to come, to the United States, a nation they see as providing the opportunity to better the lives of themselves and their children.

CHAPTER ONE

Strangers in Their Homeland

D uring the fifty-year period between the end of the American Civil War in 1865 and the outbreak of World War I in 1914, 35 million immigrants came to the United States, one of the largest waves of immigration in American history. Among these new arrivals were millions of Russians who made the long treacherous journey to seek a better life.

The Decision to Leave

Many Russians left their homeland because of unbearable poverty and lack of work. Most were peasants who lived in small villages called mirs. In these mirs, they la-bored as farmers on land that the village commonly owned together, an almost universal practice throughout Russia. Land that could be farmed was divided into sections according to the soil quality and the distance from the village. Each section was then divided among and rented by adults living in the village. The strips of land varied in size, measuring anywhere from nine to twelve feet wide and could be several hundred yards in length. A household might have anywhere from thirty to fifty of such strips of land, which were scattered around the village.

This system not only helped the villagers pay their share of rents and taxes back to the village, it was also designed to make sure that the good farming land was divided equally among them. Periodically, the village would take a census, or property and population survey, to see if the land needed to be redistributed based on changes in households. As the population of Russia increased, the availability of land decreased, causing many to go without any means of support for themselves or their families.

Those who had few prospects of acquiring land often ventured to Russian cities, where life was little better than what they had left behind in the mir. Factory work meant twelve-hour workdays (or longer) often spent in unsanitary and dangerous conditions. Wages were low, and families in the cities frequently shared one-room

A young Russian peasant prepares to leave for his mandatory enlistment in the czar's army.

apartments in order to pay rent and buy food. Opportunities to get even a basic education were nonexistent for most Russians, as was professional medical care. Those were luxuries only the wealthy could afford.

Russian men also had to serve a mandatory term of enlistment in the czar's army, and all Russian subjects were under constant scrutiny from the secret police, who could imprison anyone they wanted for real or alleged crimes. In some cases, people were exiled to Siberia, a vast frigid area of eastern Russia, never to be seen again. In addition, taxes were high, and if one could not pay, the government might seize what few belongings and little property the person owned. Many people reasoned that leaving everything behind to begin a new life in America certainly could be no worse than the lives they led in Russia.

The Russian Jews

Although most of Russia's populace suffered from poverty and fear of the government, there was one group that faced particularly hard times: the Russian Jews. Thus, of the millions of Russians who immigrated to the United States between 1880 and 1914, approximately 75 percent were Jewish.

Historians have argued over the primary reasons that drove Russian Jews to come to America. Some claim that it was because of the growing anti-Semitism in Russia, while others believe the dominant cause of the migration was poverty. There is no doubt, however, that the majority of Russian Jews who came to the United States,

Russian soldiers watch as Jews are assaulted on the streets of Kiev.

like other Russians, did so in the hopes of finding better opportunities.

Unlike many of the Russians who settled in the United States, the Russian Jews were more urbanized than non-Jewish Russian immigrants; in fact, less than 3 percent were engaged in agriculture. More than 30 percent were in some sort of business (such as peddling or shopkeeping), and an additional 40 percent were involved in some aspect of mining and manufacturing, particularly the production of clothing. In part because of restrictions placed on Jewish education and barriers to Jewish entry into certain occupations, only a tiny minority, about 3 percent, were doctors or lawyers.

Strangers in Their Homeland

By 1850, the Russian empire was vast. It stretched from Germany to Japan, covering one-sixth of the land surface of the earth. Of the approximately 70 million people living within the Russian borders in 1860, a small minority, about 3 million, were Jewish.

Like many Western Europeans, the Russians never really welcomed the Jews, whom they subjected to persecution of all kinds. In 1504, during the reign of Czar Ivan III, authorities accused a number of Jews of trying to convert the residents of the city of Novgorod to Judaism. Found guilty, these unfortunates were burned at the stake. Ivan's successor, Ivan IV, barred Jewish merchants from entering the city of Moscow during his reign. In 1742, Czarina Elizabeth attempted to rid Russia of Jews simply by banishing them from the country. When told that if her plan succeeded, Russian trade would suffer, she reportedly answered, "I do not want any benefit from the enemies of Christ."[1] In addition to these restrictions, the Russian government placed a quota on the number of Jewish students who could attend Russian secondary schools and universities.

The Pale of Settlement

By the mid–eighteenth century, the "Jewish problem" had, from the point of view of the Russian czars, become more serious. In 1772, and again in 1793 and 1795, Russia, under the rule of Catherine the Great, began annexing, or taking, large portions of Poland, a country on Russia's western border. In the process of acquiring Polish territory, the Russians also increased their population, including an additional 1 million Jews.

Although a small minority of the new Russian population, these Jewish residents were far from inconspicuous. In Poland, many had worked as craftsmen, tax collectors, merchants, and professionals. Moreover, the Jewish population in many of the Polish cities the Russians seized was as high as 70 percent, which meant a sizable increase in the overall Jewish population of the Russian empire. The increase also called for Catherine and future rulers of Russia to contain their newest residents.

To manage their new Jewish subjects, the czars resorted to discriminatory and repressive practices. In 1772, for instance, Catherine the Great issued a decree that permitted

Catherine the Great and other Russian czars discriminated against Jews.

all non-Jews in the former Polish territories to retain their civil rights, regardless of where they lived. Jews, on the contrary, were able to keep their civil rights only if they remained in the communities where they had lived before the partition of Poland. The law, in effect, prevented Jews from relocating. The Russian government then forced Jews from other parts of Russia to move to the former Polish territory, now divided into twenty-five provinces that extended from the Black Sea in the south to the Baltic Sea in the north. In ensuing years, this area became a specifically defined pale, or district, separated from the surrounding country. For Jews to live, or even to venture, beyond the pale was difficult, if not strictly forbidden. As a result of these restrictions, the area to which the Jews were confined became increasingly crowded and impoverished.

In three decrees issued during the years 1783, 1791, and 1794, Catherine the Great restricted the commercial rights of Jews to those areas that had been recently annexed. This often meant that Jewish merchants and craftsmen could sell only to Jewish customers. These actions destroyed the livelihood of more than one-third of the Jewish population. By taking away the Jews' ability to work as merchants or craftsmen, Catherine hoped to force them into farming or agricultural work. Her plan failed, though, because the supply of available land in the pale was diminishing rapidly.

Life in the Pale

The typical Jewish community in the pale was the *shtetl,* or village, which usually consisted of a few thousand residents. At the center of village life were the synagogue and the market. In the *shtetl,* many Jews earned their living as shopkeepers, peddlers, or artisans, and often an entire family helped out with the work.

Poverty remained a persistent problem. Over time, as the Jewish population, which constituted about one-ninth of the entire population of the pale, increased due to high birth rates, the number of Jews living in poverty-ridden and overcrowded conditions also grew. With available land at a premium and the high numbers of Jews unable to make a living, by the end of the nineteenth century, the Jewish population

in the pale settlements had become so poor that approximately one-third relied on some form of aid from Jewish welfare organizations to survive.

The Policy of "Official Nationality"

Nicholas I, who became czar in 1825, instituted a new policy that added even further hardship for the Jews. Termed "official nationality," the policy was Nicholas's attempt to implant the idea of Russian superiority in the minds of his subjects. This philosophy, based on the supremacy of Russian culture, the autocratic rule of the czar, and the authority of the state church, the Russian Orthodox Church, explicitly excluded the Jews and identified them as a threat to Russia's

The policies of Nicholas I made life even harder for Russian Jews.

internal security and social peace. To enforce this policy, Nicholas established an agency called the Third Section, made up of secret police and spies who monitored the activities of his subjects.

Nicholas also waged a war of oppression against the Jews, imposing a number of harsh and rigid laws that applied only to them. In 1827, for instance, Nicholas instituted a new law that required all adult Jewish males to serve a mandatory twenty-five-year term of military service. For those who could afford it, there were alternatives. Wealthy Jews could pay a fee to free themselves and their sons from this obligation. The poor, however, had no choice. If they tried to escape service, soldiers often seized them and forced them to enlist in the army.

Perhaps the most appalling of the military restrictions placed on Jews was the conscription, or enlistment, of young Jewish boys between the ages of twelve and eighteen. Some of these boys were sent directly to military barracks where the soldiers alternately brutalized and neglected them. Others went to Orthodox schools for compulsory instruction in the Russian Orthodox faith. In many villages, young boys were sent into the army as a means of keeping fathers and husbands home with their families.

In the twenty-nine years that this practice continued, between thirty and fifty thousand Jewish boys served in the Russian army's special units known as cantonist battalions. Thousands of others died during their enlistment from hunger, neglect, the brutal army life, or as victims of war. Those who survived had little to look forward to, for these early enlistments did not count toward their mandatory twenty-five-year military service as adults. To keep their sons out of the hands of the military kidnappers, known as *khapers,* desperate parents sometimes deliberately maimed or crippled them, thereby making them unfit for duty. Alexander Herzen, who later became one of the leading members in the Russian revolutionary movement, encountered a group of cantonists in 1835. Later, in trying to describe the scene, he wrote,

[It] was one of the most awful sights I have even seen. Pale, exhausted, with frightened faces, they stood in thick, clumsy, soldier's overcoats . . . fixing, helpless, pitiful eyes on the garrison, soldiers who were roughly getting them into ranks. The white lips, the blue rings under their eyes bore witness to fever or chill. And these sick children, without care or kindness, exposed to the raw wind that blows unobstructed from the Arctic Ocean were going to their graves.[2]

A Brief Respite

Some of the hardships the Russian Jews had endured began to ease in 1855 when Alexander II succeeded his father to the throne. During his reign, Alexander implemented a number of reforms that brought fundamental changes to Russian society, including the emancipation of the serfs, or peasants, in 1861. For Russian Jews, the most encouraging sign that circumstances were changing came in 1859, when on the fourth anniversary of his coronation, Alexander repealed the hated cantonist system. Alexander relaxed the restrictions of

A Misunderstood People

Throughout European history, Jews had been subjected to recurrent persecution and subjugation, mostly as the result of religious intolerance. Anti-Semitism, in fact, had a long and bloody history in Europe. Since the Middle Ages, Christians had blamed the Jews for the death of Christ, which provoked terrible anger and hatred. Many Christian kingdoms enacted laws designed to curtail Jewish religious freedom when it appeared to threaten Christian authority. For instance, Christians accused Jews of torturing and crucifying Christian children in order to use their blood in religious ceremonies. They also spread rumors that Jews poisoned wells to kill Christians, worshiped Satan, and organized a secret government that conspired to destroy Christianity.

Although some popes and bishops condemned these anti-Semitic fables and sought to protect Jews from mob violence, anti-Semitism remained popular among the European masses. Periodically, mobs humiliated, tortured, and massacred Jews, and rulers expelled Jews from their kingdoms. Often prevented from owning land and excluded from certain professions, medieval Jews concentrated in trade and money lending, occupations that the

Catholic Church condemned and that thus generated even greater hostility toward the Jews.

By the nineteenth century, however, as a result of the influence of the liberal ideals of the Enlightenment and the French Revolution, Jews gained legal equality in most European countries. They achieved remarkable success as entrepreneurs, bankers, lawyers, journalists, physicians, scientists, scholars, and performers. Still, most European Jews were poor, and many ultimately fled to the United States to escape the desperate poverty in which they lived.

The myth of Jewish world conspiracy reached its culmination in a notorious forgery titled *The Protocols of the Elders of Zion*. Written in France during the 1890s by an unknown author employed by the Russian secret police, *The Protocols* sought to justify the czar's anti-Semitic policies. The forger concocted a fantastic tale of an alleged meeting of the Jewish elders at a cemetery in Prague. In these eerie surroundings, the book claimed the elders plotted to take over the world. This story, along with the increased legal restrictions on the Russian Jews, only helped intensify the growing anti-Semitic feelings throughout Russia.

the pale settlements as well. Jews who were trained in useful and needed occupations such as artisans, doctors, lawyers, and merchants were allowed to settle outside the pale boundaries.

The permission to move and live freely held great appeal, and eligible Jews quickly left the pale settlements. As a result, Jewish communities in Russian cities like St. Petersburg, Moscow, and Odessa grew rapidly,

Russian leaders used the assassination of Czar Alexander II on March 1, 1881 as an excuse to increase persecution of the country's Jews.

as Jews began participating more fully in Russian life. And increased industrial development in these cities created opportunities for Jewish entrepreneurs, particularly in banking, export trading, mining, and the construction of railroads. Alexander also instituted reforms that made it easier for Russian Jews to enroll in Russian schools and universities. Although these reforms did little to aid the thousands of Jews who struggled in poverty or who would never leave the pale, they represented a promising start.

Not everyone, though, was pleased with Alexander's reforms. The sudden appearance of more Jewish lawyers, journalists, and businessmen brought a sharp and critical reaction from many Russians, rich and poor. Then on March 1, 1881, Alexander II was assassinated by a terrorist's bomb when returning to his home at the Winter Palace in St. Petersburg. As a result of the czar's assassination, many Russian Jews

had dark premonitions about the future. One Jewish diarist wrote,

It was on March 1, 1881, that the sun which had risen over Jewish life in the eighteen-fifties was suddenly eclipsed. Alexander the II was assassinated on the bank of the Catherine Canal in Saint Petersburg. The hand that had signed the edict freeing the sixty million serfs had become motionless. The mouth that uttered the great word "Emancipation" was silenced forever. And the salvation hoped for by the people receded far into the distance.[3]

A Dark Time

Although Alexander's son and successor, Czar Alexander III, received several prominent Jewish citizens on the day of his father's funeral, few held much hope that the Russian Jews would be spared violence following the czar's death. A writer in a Jewish newspaper noted that "in the reaction which [is] sure to come on the murder of the Czar, the Jews will lose some of the privileges gained during the reign of Alexander II. . . . God help them if but the faintest shadow of suspicion rests upon any Jews for . . . the conspiracy."[4]

To the horror of many Jews, one of the six conspirators later arrested in the assassination plot did turn out to be a Jewish woman. Thus, the events following the murder of Czar Alexander II dashed all hopes the Russian Jews had for additional improvements in their situation. Not only did the assassination occur in an atmosphere of great social unrest, but it also offered those who distrusted and hated the Jews an excuse to implicate them in Alexander's death and thus exact savage vengeance.

Thanks in part to Alexander III, anti-Semitism in Russia again became respectable, legal, and increasingly violent. Alexander often denounced the Jewish people, blaming them for his father's death, and once stated that "In my heart, I am very glad when they beat the Jews, even though this practice cannot be permitted."[5] But permit it he did. Even though his advisers occasionally managed to control the violence for short periods of time, the dam of resentment and hatred had burst.

A Tragic End

Historians have vivid and reliable accounts of Czar Alexander II's assassination in 1881. One eyewitness, Peter Kropotkin, an officer in the Russian army, was with Alexander the day he died. In this account taken from Readings in Modern European History, *Kropotkin describes the events after the bombing of Alexander's carriage.*

It is known how it happened. A bomb was thrown under his iron-clad carriage to stop it. . . . Rysakoff, who flung the bomb, was arrested on the spot. Then, although the coachman of the Tsar earnestly advised him not to get out, saying that he could drive him still in the slightly damaged carriage, he insisted upon alighting. . . . He approached Rysakoff and asked him something; and as he passed close by another young man . . . threw a bomb between himself and Alexander II, so that both of them should be killed. . . . There Alexander II lay upon the snow, profusely bleeding, abandoned by every one of his followers. All had disappeared. It was cadets, returning from parade, who lifted the suffering Tsar from the snow and put him in a sledge [sled] covering his shivering body with a cadet mantle [a coat] and his bare head with a cadet cap. And it was one of the terrorists . . . with a bomb wrapped in a paper under his arm, who, at the risk of being arrested on the spot and hanged, rushed with the cadets to the help of the wounded man. . . . Thus ended the tragedy of Alexander II's life.

"The Pogroms Were All Around Us"

The first of these incidents occurred on April 11, 1881, in Yelizavetgrad, a small town located 150 miles northeast of Odessa.

A group of youths began spreading a rumor that the czar had officially given permission for Orthodox Russians to beat up the Jewish residents of the town and take their property. Alarmed by this turn of events,

Jews flee violence in nineteenth-century Russia.

Fiddler on the Roof

Based on the short story "Tevye and His Daughters" by Russian immigrant writer Sholom Aleichem, *Fiddler on the Roof* became one of the first musicals with a somber plot line to enjoy commercial success. Not only did the play deal with serious issues such as persecution, poverty, and the struggle to hold on to established beliefs and traditions, it also explored how one Jewish family managed to survive during a particularly chaotic period in Russian history. Initially criticized for its "limited appeal" when the play first premiered in 1964, *Fiddler on the Roof* struck such a universal chord with audiences that it became, for a time, the longest-running production in the history of Broadway.

Set in 1905, the story takes place in Anatevka, a small Jewish village in Russia. The plot revolves around the dairyman Tevye and his attempts to preserve his family traditions in the face of a changing world. When his eldest daughter begs him to let her marry a poor tailor rather than the middle-aged butcher whom he has already chosen for her, Tevye must decide between his daughter's

happiness and the beloved traditions that keep a hostile world at bay. Meanwhile, other forces at work in the village threaten to destroy the way of life Teyve is trying to preserve. The play and the film adapted from it remain among the most popular musicals ever produced, and they captured for many Americans a sense of what life might have been like in czarist Russia.

An actor performs a scene from Fiddler on the Roof, *one of the most popular musicals ever produced.*

Jewish leaders appealed to the local authorities for protection. A detachment of soldiers was immediately sent, but recalled three days later when nothing had happened. As soon as the soldiers withdrew, the troubles began again.

On Wednesday, April 15, 1881, a fight broke out in a tavern between the Jewish owner and a non-Jewish customer. Shoving the customer into the street, the owner met up with an angry mob. Some cried, "The Zhids [Jews] are beating up our people!"[6]

Another fight broke out, and some members of the crowd began beating any Jews who were happening by; others, meanwhile, forced their way into the tavern and stole alcohol. According to one contemporary account, "The rioters proceeded to the Jewish quarter, and commenced a systematic destruction of the shops and warehouses . . . [then] proceeded to attack the dwellings of the Jews and to wreck the synagogue."[7]

The violence continued throughout the next day, with additional damage done to Jewish shops and homes. Even with the help of the military, which Jewish leaders and village officials had summoned to restore order, the Jewish residents were powerless against their attackers. By that evening, hundreds of shops and homes had been destroyed. One Jewish man had been killed, and a number of Jewish women had been raped.

Violence and unrest continued. Riots broke out in cities and towns throughout the pale. The Russian government did little to protect the Jews, and Russian officials seemed largely indifferent to their plight. In some cases, government agents even showed sympathy for those who had instigated the violence, blaming the Jews for provoking the incidents.

No Jew was safe. Jewish residents lived in fear for their lives. In the year following Alexander II's assassination, the Russian government carried out more than two hundred pogroms, or massacres, primarily in the southwestern regions where the pales of settlement were located. During that same period, more than forty Jews were murdered; thousands of others were deprived of their property, rendered homeless and penniless. Russian civilians and the Cossacks, an elite military unit that participated in many of the pogroms, did not hesitate to destroy entire Jewish settlements.

In 1881, Shmuel Goldman was a young boy living in a small village near the Vistula River (a region now in Poland). He remembered that "the pogroms were all around us." On one particular day, the furious ringing of the village church bells signaled to Goldman that something was wrong. He later described the sight:

> The soldiers on horseback would tear through the town and leave dead Jews behind. . . . All night we stayed huddling together . . . and heard the terrible noises outside—horses, screams, shouts. We were afraid to light the lamps or the stove. . . . Who knows what would have happened without the warning? As it is, the soldiers tore up the Jewish streets, broke windows, threw the furniture out. We came out into the sparkling sunshine and the streets were white like winter. Everywhere were feathers from where those Cossacks cut up our featherbeds.[8]

The Temporary Laws

In May 1882, Czar Alexander III decreed the so-called Temporary Laws that ushered in a new period of Jewish discrimination and persecution, which officially lasted until 1917. One law reduced the size of the pale of settlement by 10 percent, forcing many Jews to leave their homes. Jews were once again prohibited from living in villages and from buying or selling property outside prescribed areas. Jews were also denied jobs in the Russian civil service and forbidden to trade on Sundays and Christian holidays.

Eight years later, the anti-Semitic campaigns intensified after Alexander III and his family survived a railway accident. The head of the Orthodox Church and the czar's spiritual advisor, K. Pobedonostsev, interpreted the czar's escape from death as a sign of divine intervention from God to turn away from the path of reform. Alexander took this advice to mean that it was permissible to turn his back on the Russian Jews and abandon them to their fate.

As a result, even more laws restricting the Jewish people were adopted. In 1887, the number of Jewish students permitted to enter secondary school in the pale was restricted to 10 percent of the total enrollment. In 1891, a decree was issued ordering the Jewish residents of Moscow, many of whom had resided in the city since 1865, to be expelled. Within months, approximately twenty thousand people were forced to give up their homes and jobs to be deported, many of them in chains, to the overcrowded pale, where 4 million Jews already resided.

With the death of Alexander III in 1894, the Jews hoped that his successor, Nicholas II, would intervene on their behalf; in fact, for a period after the coronation of the new czar, there were fewer incidents of violence directed against the Jews. Many Jewish

Flags for the Czar

One of the most fascinating accounts of life in the pale settlements came from a young Jewish girl named Mary Antin, who recounted growing up in the village of Polotzk during the late nineteenth century. In this excerpt from her autobiography quoted in the Modern History Sourcebook "Mary Antin: A Little Jewish Girl in the Russian Pale," Antin recounts how the Jews, persecuted as they were by Czar Alexander III, were still required to pay him allegiance.

The czar was always sending us commands,—you shall not do this and you shall not do that,—till there was very little left that we might do, except pay tribute and die. On a royal birthday every house must fly a flag, or the owner would be dragged to a police station and be fined twenty-five rubles. A decrepit old woman, who lived all alone in a tumble-down shanty, supported by the charity of the neighborhood, crossed her paralyzed hands one day when flags were ordered up, and waited for her doom, because she had no flag. The vigilant policeman kicked the door open with his great boot, took the last pillow from the bed, sold it, and hoisted a flag above the rotten roof.

families went about their lives, difficult as they may have become, in relative peace and security.

But the constant specter of the pogroms once more became a reality in 1903. That year alone, reports estimated that at least forty-nine Jews were murdered and more than five hundred injured. The violence continued off and on for years, sweeping through large cities and small towns, with some of the worst incidents occurring in Odessa, Kishinev, Kiev, and Yelizavet-grad. Many Jews had had enough. The time had come to take action.

CHAPTER TWO

Coming to America

For Russian immigrants, the decision to come to America was not an easy one. Nor was immigration simple to accomplish. In addition to the anguish of leaving friends, family, and familiar places behind, there was the uncertainty of what lay ahead. Still, the opportunity to escape poverty and oppression was enough to encourage many Russians to take a chance. For Russian Jews in particular, leaving Russia meant getting away not only from the pale settlement but from the constant fear of harassment and violence that marked so much of their lives. Surely, coming to America could not be any worse.

Before they could depart for America, however, the immigrants had to get permission to leave Russia. Then, whether by foot, rail, or covered wagon, the travelers set out on a journey that took weeks, perhaps even months, to complete.

Permission to Leave

It had always been difficult for Russians to leave their homeland. Throughout the nineteenth century, for instance, the government's mandatory military service, and the country's high taxes, made it impossible for many to leave the country. Government restrictions on travel inside Russia also hindered people from trying to get away. Some took drastic measures. One man who refused to join the Russian army jumped into the river bordering Russia and Germany and swam to freedom. Another immigrant walked to Poland, where he bribed the Polish border guards to let him enter the country.

For the few immigrants who did receive permission to leave, the process of securing the necessary documentation often took months to complete. First, the prospective immigrant needed to fill out a passport application, which was available only through the governor of the province where he or she resided. For many, this was a near-impossible task, because few Russian peasants were able to read or write. For those who could fill out the application, the next barrier was the payment of a fee, money that many Russians did not have.

Whether leaving Russia legally or illegally, money often proved to be an enormous problem for the immigrants. Transportation needed to be arranged and guides hired to help with the journey. Forged documents might also have to be bought, and officials frequently demanded bribes in order to let people slip through. Boat fare to the United States, on average, cost ten to fifteen dollars a person, and for those trying to leave with families, this amounted to a staggering sum of money.

Sneaking Away

One of the first and largest groups to leave Russia during the late nineteenth century were the Russian Jews. In May 1881, shortly after the first pogrom at Yelizavetgrad, the London *Daily Telegraph* reported that Russian Jews "are removing from the disturbed districts as fast as they can."[9] Many, now realizing how dangerous it had become to be a Jew in Russia, saw that there was only one real way to escape from their persecution: to leave the country forever.

The biggest question facing many Russian Jews was where they should go to start their new lives. Some left for Austria, which bordered the pale settlements. Others scattered throughout Western Europe in such places as France and Germany. Many others, though, looked across the Atlantic to the United States.

Getting to America was not easy. For many Russian Jews, the first stage of the journey meant getting safely to the Austrian province of Galicia, located in the northeastern corner of the country. The border was poorly patrolled, so crossing without a

Jews fled Russia to escape violence and persecution.

passport was relatively easy. In Austria, there were many Jewish communities, making it easier for immigrants who entered the country illegally to blend in and hide from authorities. From any one of these small Galician villages, Jews made their way to Brody, a city of almost twenty-five thousand residents, many of them Jewish, and thus began in earnest their long, hopeful journey to America.

Some Russian Jews relied on professional smugglers, or guides, who, for a price, aided Jews in safely crossing the borders without being detected. Many years later, one young man, Alexander Harkey, described his experiences escaping from Russia in 1882:

> Our first destination was a small city in Lithuania near the Prussian [German-Austrian] border. . . . There we found a Jew engaged in border crossing. We contracted with him to cross into Prussia at a price of three rubles a head. Toward evening the man brought a large wagon which took us as far as the border district. There we got off the wagon and the man left us . . . to bargain on our behalf with one of the district's residents. . . . After an hour, our border crosser returned with a Christian man and both quietly ordered us to come along. Trembling mightily, we followed them. They led us into Prussia. The border area was filled with wells of water and slime. . . . Finally after wandering about for half an hour we came to the city of Eydtkühnen in Prussia. The short time had seemed to us an eternity.[10]

Bodies for Dollars

Among the greatest benefactors of "American fever" (the immigrants' desire to come to the United States) were the many shipping companies that operated throughout the nineteenth and early twentieth centuries. The absence of safety or business regulations allowed these companies to take advantage of the many immigrants who were desperate to get to the United States. Unscrupulous travel agents sold fake tickets to people or simply did not show up at the promised time and place with the needed tickets.

Other companies, conscious of the great profits to be made, crowded their ships with immigrants they knew were too ill to be allowed into the United States. Although these companies had to pay for the immigrants' return passage, they did not have to take them back to the original point of departure. This often meant that some immigrants ended up in foreign countries with no resources or anyone they could turn to for help. After increasing pressure from the U.S. government, shipping lines were required to institute their own medical examinations to prevent potentially unfit prospects from making the journey.

Journey by Rail

No matter how the new Jewish or non-Jewish immigrants left Russia, even as they crossed into Lithuania, Prussia, or Austria, they were still a long way from their destination. Those who traveled by train found themselves crowded into passenger cars in which men and women were often separated; young children usually stayed with the female members of the family. In the case of the Russian Jews who were going to the United States, an escort from one of the many Jewish relief and charitable organizations usually traveled along too. The immigrants were expected to do as their escort instructed. One group of Jewish travelers on their way to America was told, "With every transport from Brody to Hamburg [Germany] an escort goes along. He holds all your railway tickets, and all who go with him must grant him *full authority to act* without discussion of the matter, whether it has to do with money or provisions."[11]

George Price, a Russian Jew who emigrated with his parents in 1882, remembered their departure from Brody:

> There was an immense crowd. We waited at the [train] station about six hours, and were finally admitted to the platform. They assigned a compartment to ten passengers and gave each of us a loaf of bread and two eggs. The [train] agent walked from car to car and bade the emigrants farewell.[12]

There was nothing luxurious about this trip. The wooden seats were hard, with several people jammed uncomfortably together to avoid sitting on the already crowded floor. At night, if they were lucky, the passengers might find a small space on the floor where they would sleep, their belongings clutched tightly to their chests. The passengers had food and water only if they had brought it with them, and once it was gone they had either to depend on the kindness of their traveling companions or go without. Periodically, the train would stop to take on additional cars of other immigrants, but no one was allowed to get off, even for provisions, until they reached their destination: a port city in which they would board a ship for the United States.

The Next Stage

Most of these cities—near Hamburg—were located in Germany on the North Sea. Many Jewish immigrants, whose journey to America was being paid for by a Jewish relief organization in Europe or the United States, were given explicit instructions as to what they were to do upon their arrival in the port cities. According to one relief group, upon reaching Hamburg, the immigrants were to "find a place to stay for two and a half days, in a transients' residence where you can get room and board . . . to be paid for [by] the traveler out of his own pocket."[13] In the port cities, immigrants booked passage on the next ship to America, and again, this often meant days and sometimes weeks of waiting.

In the meantime, the Russian immigrants found themselves wandering city streets, a startling experience for many who had never ventured far from their tiny villages. One immigrant, only seven at the time he and his family made their way to the United States, remembered his first impressions of the German city of Berlin, which he saw from the window of a railway car. "It seemed to my childish imagination that we were flying in fairyland," he recalled. "The twinkling lights of the street lamps appearing in all directions and my watching from the height of the elevated roof . . . left an impression on my youthful mind."[14]

While waiting for a boat, thousands of Russian immigrants stayed at one of the "villages," makeshift communities owned by the steamship companies. Up to four thousand immigrants at a time received food and lodging in these places. For many Russians, the stay in the villages was an overwhelming experience. Most had never taken a hot-water shower, seen electric lights, or experienced steam heat.

For the thousands of other immigrants, those with very little money to spend, temporary residences consisted of filthy barracks or rundown boardinghouses. Their meals were the meager rations they had brought for themselves or the stale bread and bland soup that were offered by their landlords. Other immigrants who had no money slept in the city streets.

When the ship finally arrived, the immigrants were tired of waiting and longed to begin the next phase of their journey. Before being allowed to board, however, the immigrants were given medical examinations. One woman vividly remembered her examination by the German officials:

> The Germans looked in our heads, hair by hair . . . for nits [lice]. Now a lot of the girls, the Germans cut their hair off altogether. They made them bald. . . . My sister, Margie, right

Russian Jews congregate in Germany, awaiting passage to America.

away they cut off her hair. She had beautiful hair and right away they cut it off. They didn't find anything. But they said it was for safety.[15]

Representatives of the shipping line also saw to it that all the clothing and belongings of the immigrants were fumigated and cleaned to prevent outbreaks of contagious diseases. Furthermore, the immigrants were asked a series of questions by the ship line officials, who then forwarded the responses on to American immigration officials in the United States. The immigrants' answers to these questions would be compared to the answers they gave to similar questions in America; that way officials could uncover any inconsistent or false information.

The Voyage

At last, the day arrived when the ship was ready to be boarded. People gathered at the dock area and were then crowded onto a small ferry boat that transported them directly to the large ocean liner. The majority of the Russian immigrants found themselves on ships first bound for England. From there, they would board another ship that would carry them to the United States.

On average, close to one thousand immigrants bought tickets that entitled them to occupy the "steerage" section of the ship, where they spent the rest of their journey. Traveling in steerage meant that the immigrants' tickets entitled them to a place on the lowest deck of the ship, in an area located near the bow, or front of the ship. One immigrant passenger, upon seeing the steerage

The Smell of "Ship"

One of the most distinctive aspects of the sea journey was known as the smell of "ship." The stale air, sweat, and use of soap and disinfectants on board combined to make an unusual odor. One Russian immigrant who came to the United States in 1895, quoted in Ann Novotny's Strangers at the Door: Ellis Island, Castle Garden, and the Great Migration to America, *described this peculiar phenomenon.*

[It was] a . . . phenomenon known to all transatlantic travelers of those days as the smell of "ship." This pervasive, insidious odor, a distillation of bilge [sewage] and a number of less identifiable putrescences, settled on one's person, clothes, and luggage, and stayed there forever, impervious to changes of habitat, clothing, and the cleansing agents available to the poor. It was many years before I realized that only steerage passengers smelled of "ship." . . . One *expected* arrivals from Europe to smell of "ship." So much so that on visits to the homes of neighbors, one could tell at once by the pervading smell . . . that they were entertaining guests from abroad.

Immigrants huddle together in steerage on the voyage to America. Because they had little money, most Russian immigrants had to travel in steerage.

section for the first time, described it as "the dreadful, salty suffocating smell of the cellar . . . filled with shallow wooden boxes that they called beds."[16] Another Russian immigrant likened his quarters to "a large egg crate, with three tiers of cubicles for bunks and with just enough room in the center to move about before climbing in and out of our beds."[17] But steerage was the cheapest form of sea travel, and without it many immigrants could have never afforded the journey to America.

Life Below Deck

Conditions in steerage were miserable. To make as much money as possible, the ship companies booked as many passengers as their vessels could accommodate and then some. Some companies even refitted cattle ships to carry immigrants to the United States. One Jewish immigrant wrote of the first time he saw his quarters for the trip:

> We were all herded together in a dark, filthy compartment in the steerage. We learned that our vessel had formerly been a cattle ship and had just been converted into a passenger boat. Our compartment was enormously large, and wooden bunks had been put up in two tiers, one on top of the other. Here men, women and children were herded together.[18]

Anywhere from forty to fifty persons crowded into one room with no ventilation other than the fresh air that escaped from the hatchway through which they had entered. On some voyages, each person received a stack of straw, a quilt, and a dipper for water. Sometimes cots were handed out for sleeping. On some ships, women and small children resided in one section, while men were taken to another. Other ships had "marriage quarters" where families and small children could stay. Regardless, the odor of sweaty bodies intermingled with sickness and the heat made breathing difficult. And the water that was available often tasted bad and gave people stomach aches.

Many of the immigrants also suffered from terrible seasickness for the entire trip. One young Russian immigrant remembered his first night aboard the ship. Upon hearing his bunkmate becoming sick, he said he arose:

> With the greatest caution because I didn't want to be hit by the contents of the stomach being steadily disgorged by my upper neighbor. When I got up and walked by the women's quarters, I heard more screaming. Other men were up to help the sick. In a little while our whole stateroom was filled with sick and "nurses." There was a running to the sailors for water and to the doctor for help and medicine. Instead of water and medicine we received a bawling out for disturbing their sleep.[19]

Meals in steerage were taken at long common tables, on which people ate from large bowls. Many immigrants often could not eat, though, because of the terrible smells. As one traveler later remembered, that turned out to be a blessing because there was often not enough food to go around. Another immigrant remembered coming upon a table loaded with food of all types but being unable to eat. He wrote:

> It was not because there was any lack of quantity. The tables were loaded with bread, butter, herring, cake and potatoes in their skins and we were free to take as much as we wished. But the trouble was that we could not put the stuff in our mouths. The butter smelled like old wax, the herring like raw fresh fish. The cake was mouldy. The bread and potatoes without good reason had a nauseating taste.[20]

During the voyage, there were few diversions available for the immigrants. On sunny days, many would crowd the lower deck to take advantage of the fresh air and sunshine. Some people sang songs from the old country, while others smoked pipes and played cards. Children scampered around the deck making new friends and marveling at the ship's technology. Immigrants from other countries might try to strike up conversations with each other. Bernard Weinstein, a Russian Jew, remembered these occasions with great fondness:

> We spent most of the time on deck looking at the sea and talking about America. In the evenings when the sky was clear, we would gaze at the enchanting colors of sunset—Then, as the

magical hues extinguished themselves one by one, our hearts would reach out with longing. We would then gather together and sing Russian folk songs.[21]

When the weather turned stormy, though, everyone went below decks. For those unfamiliar with ocean travel, a storm at sea was a terrifying experience. One immigrant remembered encountering a storm of great ferocity on his voyage to America in 1882. As the ship was battered about, he and his traveling companions waited for the storm to subside:

We were not able to stand or sit and if we attempted to lie down in our bunks we were shaken out. Trunks, benches and other objects slid from one side of the ship to the other. . . . It was frightening to see the huge waves black as ink which appeared ready to swallow the entire ship.[22]

In spite of the terrible traveling conditions, shortages, and inclement weather, there was an enthusiasm shared among many of the immigrants as each day went by. As one young Russian exclaimed about the difficulties of the journey, "Who cared? We were going to America!"[23]

America!

After a voyage lasting anywhere from two weeks to a month, the ship finally reached

Immigrants point out the Statue of Liberty, the symbol of freedom in their new home.

port in New York City. For many, the first glimpse of America was overwhelming. One immigrant later wrote of his first reaction upon entering the harbor, "To the west boats and ships passed at regular intervals and a few lighthouses were in sight. It is impossible to describe the joy and excitement. . . . We beheld with our own eyes the magnificent shores of America."[24]

The immigrants first glimpsed the majestic Statue of Liberty, welcoming ships from all over the world into New York Harbor. Beyond that, there stood in the distance a group of buildings that housed the country's largest immigration processing center: Ellis Island.

Ellis Island

After they disembarked from the ship, the immigrants were packed onto a small ferry boat that took them to the main buildings at Ellis Island. Once the ferry boat reached its destination, attendants hurried the Russians, and thousands of other immigrants from all over the world, into a large, red brick building. Upon entering, the immigrants found themselves in a large, dark-tiled entrance corridor, where they were directed toward a flight of stairs. Watching them as they climbed the stairs were officials from the U.S. Public Health Service who were scanning the crowd for individuals who were having trouble climbing the stairs, a possible signal of illness or disability; both were grounds for deportation.

At the top of the stairs, the immigrants were then directed to doors that led them into the Registry Hall, a large room divided into a maze of open passageways. The first stop was a visit with a doctor from the U.S. Public Health Service. As the immigrants came before him, an interpreter asked questions about their age, health, and destination, while the doctor examined their faces, necks, hands, and hair. Immigrants who were identified as having visible health problems had their clothing marked with chalk; for example, an "H" meant heart trouble, an "X" meant that the person was mentally defective, and "Pg" symbolized pregnancy.

After the first health inspection, the immigrant then moved on to another medical officer known as the "eye man." Standing at the end of the line, these officials inspected the eyes of every immigrant. The eye examination, though quick, was thorough, as one doctor's description shows:

[The doctor] looks carefully at the eyeball in order to detect signs of defect and disease of that organ and quickly everts [looks under] the upper lids in search of conjunctivitis and trachoma [two contagious diseases of the inner eye]. . . . Squint, bulging eyes, the wearing of eye glasses, clumsiness, and other signs on the part of the alien, will be sufficient cause for him to be chalk-marked "Vision." He will then be taken out of the line by the attendant and his vision will be carefully examined.[25]

After their eyes were examined and cleaned to prevent the outbreak of disease, the immigrants moved on to the next step. Those who had been "chalked" were taken to an area where doctors conducted a more

The Registry Hall

During their time at Ellis Island, all Russian immigrants passed through the Registry Hall, a room that was for many the largest they had ever seen. It was here that immigrants moved through open passageways like a maze and awaited questions from immigration officials that determined whether they would be allowed to stay or would be sent back home. Measuring two hundred feet long and one hundred feet wide, with a fifty-six-foot vaulted ceiling, the room, on any given day, had thousands of people pass through on their way to their new lives in America. Outside were a series of wooden benches where immigrants spent hours awaiting their chance to go in. Off to one side of the Registry Hall were dormitories for those individuals who needed further medical attention, were quarantined, or were detained until they could be sent back home. Conditions were overcrowded, dirty, and noisy.

For some, the experience at Ellis Island was not a pleasant one. Baroness Mara de Lilier-Steinhall, quoted in David M. Brownstone, Irene M. Franck, and Douglass Brownstone's book, Island of Hope, Island of Tears, described her time at Ellis Island in 1923:

> The prisons conducted by the Soviet government are not more dirty or more favorable for disease than the [Registry] hall on Ellis Island where I was confined with a thousand men and women. I have been through worse things . . . but I have never been forced to live in such filth and under such unhygienic conditions.

The Registry Hall on Ellis Island was the first stop for most immigrants to America.

thorough medical examination to determine the state of their health and any specific ailments they might have. It was estimated that 15 to 20 percent of each group of immigrants to Ellis Island were found to have medical problems of some sort.

Immigrants who were certified as being healthy then awaited their next and final step. Here, the last test awaited all who had successfully made it from their village to the port cities to the ship and across the Atlantic to America. Each person appeared before an-

After passing through various inspections, immigrants finally left Ellis Island to begin their new lives in America.

other inspector, and an interpreter asked a series of questions. The questions were used as a means of determining whether the immigrants had sufficient resources (such as family, relatives, or a job) that would allow them to stay in America. The questions were also used to identify people who might pose a threat to the security of the country or who might be considered dangerous to the public.

Finally, if the immigrants answered the questions to the satisfaction of the officials, they were allowed to leave, their "landing cards" (documents that certified they were in America legally) in hand. Those with money went to the Money Exchange to trade their rubles for dollars. Others tried to track down any baggage they may have brought with them on the trip over. Still others found their way to the railroad windows to purchase tickets to travel west. Their new life in America had begun.

CHAPTER THREE

The Three Waves of Russian Immigration

From the end of World War I until the 1980s, there were what historians have termed three waves, or groups, of Russian immigration. These waves followed the earlier mass exodus of Russian Jews and are different in many ways. One of the biggest differences is that the later groups left Russia not to escape the czar but to flee the Communist regime that ruled the country and several surrounding states from 1917 until the 1990s. Another difference is that, unlike the early Russian Jews who harbored resentment of the czarist regime, the immigrants who left after 1917 had a strong attachment to their homeland.

The first wave of immigration, which lasted from the Russian Revolution in 1917 until 1928, brought thousands of Russians to the United States who were fleeing the devastation of the revolution and World War I. Unlike earlier immigrants, the Russians who came after World War I tended to be from the middle and upper classes, whose property the Communist government had seized and whose lives it had threatened. By coming to the United States, this group hoped to escape the unpredictable and dangerous world of Communist oppression in Soviet Russia.

The second wave of Russian immigrants, which began during the post–World

War II era, lasted roughly from 1945 until 1951. By the time World War II ended in 1945, the faces of the Russian immigrants had changed once more. This time, they were neither poor serfs nor imperiled aristocrats. Instead, they were war refugees, fleeing both a devastated country and the Soviet soldiers ordered to detain them.

Beginning in the 1960s and continuing until 1985 is the third wave of Russian immigrants. Many of these newcomers to the United States were also Russian Jews, still the victims of legal and cultural persecution, who were allowed to leave as the result of the Soviet government's relaxation of emigration laws. Others came to America as exiles and dissidents, who were considered traitors to the Soviet Union. But no matter which group these immigrants were associated with, they all came to the United States to be free.

Prelude to a Revolution

When World War I began in 1914, Russia allied with Great Britain and France to fight against Germany and Austria-Hungary. The war, which many had thought would last only a few months, became a long, bitter struggle, during which the Russians endured terrible hardships.

To aid its allies, the Russian government drafted approximately 16 million men into the army, most of them ill trained and ill equipped. Russian conscripts served their country for pitiful wages (the average Russian soldier earned only 25 cents a month; an American private, by comparison, received $33). They also found themselves fighting a war that few understood. By 1916, many Russians were looking for a way out of the conflict.

Compounding the problems of the military were the equally devastating hardships

A Relaxing of Rules

The decision in 1947 to let Soviet refugees come to America was not made lightly. A series of immigration laws passed more than two decades earlier had made entrance into the United States difficult for all immigrants from Eastern Europe. In 1921, Congress passed the Quota Act, restricting the flow of immigrants into the United States. The law was designed to stem the influx of World War I refugees into the country by limiting the number of Soviet immigrants and others from the Baltic states

to approximately ten thousand. Three years later, when the Quota Act was due to expire, Congress passed another law that further tightened the flow of immigration.

After World War II, though, the U.S. government temporarily suspended this legislation for two reasons. First, the government wished to help the thousands of refugees who needed new homes, and second, the country was facing a huge labor shortage, which new immigrants would help to overcome.

the Russian people faced at home. Because all available supplies were being sent to the armies, the civilian population faced shortages of food and heating fuel. As one historian later wrote:

As snow-clogged railways and disabled locomotives halted vital food and fuel shipments, Russian cities froze and people went hungry. Bread prices climbed by more than two percent each week . . . potatoes and cabbage by three, milk by five, and sausage by seven. . . . As in earlier less prosperous times, workers no longer ate eggs, meat, milk, and fruit and settled for watery cabbage soup and bits of black bread that became increasingly harder to come by.[26]

Resentment toward the czar and the Russian government grew to dangerous levels, as Russians blamed their leaders for their predicament. The question many people around the world pondered was not if there would be a revolution but when it would happen. "Underneath, everything is seething," wrote one Moscow newspaper editor. "The tighter the government screws down the top on the caldron, the bigger the explosion is going to be."[27]

Russian soldiers surrender to German forces during World War I. Russian losses in the war contributed to the eventual Communist takeover of Russia.

Revolution!

By 1917, the Russian people had had enough and rose up against Czar Nicholas II. Violence broke out in the capital of Petrograd (formerly the city of St. Petersburg), which Russian troops refused to suppress. Many soldiers even joined the rebellion. Despite the czar's efforts to dissolve the Duma, or Russian parliament, in an attempt to stop any further political unrest, Duma members refused to comply. Instead, the Duma established a provisional, or temporary, government.

On March 15, 1917, facing a hopeless situation, Nicholas abdicated, giving up the throne that the Romanov family had held for more than three centuries. In a speech given before the Duma, Nicholas stated, "In these decisive days in the life of Russia we [the royal family] have thought that we owed to our people the close union and organisation of all its forces for the realisation of a rapid victory; for which reason, in agreement with the Imperial Duma, we have recognized that it is for the good of the country that we should abdicate the Crown of the Russian State and lay down the Supreme Power."[28]

Nicholas's abdication did not settle matters, though. For the next several months, the Russian people continued to suffer from fighting and civil unrest as various political groups competed against one another for control of the country. A number of groups—consisting of workers, soldiers, and peasants—called soviets formed. These groups later provided the basis for the Bolsheviks (Communists), who eventually rose to power.

Finally, in November 1917, the Communists, under the leadership of Vladimir Ilich Ulyanov, known as Lenin, forced the

Led by Vladimir Lenin, the communists took power in November 1917.

provisional government out of power, arrested most of its members, and established a new government in the name of the soviets. Russia became known as the Union of Soviet Socialist Republics, or the USSR, but the revolution was far from over. For the next two years, civil war raged. Alarmed at the Communist takeover of Russia, the United States and European powers sent aid and troops to help the anti-Communist forces. Yet it was the Communists in the end who prevailed.

Millions of Russians were forced to leave their country after the Communist revolution.

The First Wave: Escapees from the New Regime

Between 1917 and 1921, the year the Russian civil war ended, approximately 2 million Russians fled their country and the Communists. The ongoing threat of violence, riots, property destruction, political uncertainty, oppression, and war prompted many to seek a new home. Although many of these immigrants settled in Western Europe, with the majority going to France, almost thirty thousand traveled to the United States.

Unlike earlier Russian immigrants who were mostly poor and uneducated, these men and women were often well educated and may once have been wealthy. Many had been staunch supporters of the czar and members of the Russian aristocracy. The civil war not only disrupted their way of life but left many penniless with nowhere to turn. For those who managed to elude the hated Cheka, or secret police, there was still the threat of being sent to a labor camp in Siberia, or simply being executed for having supported the czarist regime. For many, the choice was simple: They would have to leave Russia and start over or die.

A Heartbreaking Decision

Leaving Russia, though, was just the first of many hardships. The world war, the Bolshevik revolution, and the Russian civil war had all wreaked havoc on the country. The

Russian railway system and many of the country's roads were impassable. People fleeing the secret police had to find out-of-the-way routes, often traveling on foot and at night to escape capture. Some immigrants left Russia by traveling south through Turkey and from there finding passage to the United States. Others traveled through Leningrad (formerly St. Petersburg/Petrograd) or Moscow and headed north to the city of Vladivostok. From there they crossed the Pacific, arriving in the western United States or Canada, and then headed to Vancouver, Seattle, Portland, or San Francisco.

One of the biggest obstacles facing the new immigrants upon arrival in the United States was employment. Many of these people had previously relied on servants and had neither the skills nor the temperament to work at a job that demanded punctuality, hard work, and long hours. Others who had been doctors, lawyers, or government officials in their homeland soon found to their dismay that the skills they possessed were useless or unwanted in America. Thus, they often had to apply for many of the same jobs that immigrants with no education and few skills were applying for.

Some of these upper-class immigrants fell back on what they did have in abundance: social graces. Their knowledge of good manners and how to behave in upper-class society gained them access to service jobs as maids, butlers, valets, and chauffeurs in private homes. Others worked as doormen and waiters in fine hotels and restaurants. For those who had taught school in Russia, learning English often led to teaching jobs. One Russian princess who was gifted in needlework sold quilts, and a former officer in the czar's army opened a riding academy.

Another problem facing the new Russian immigrants was their overwhelming homesickness. Despite the terrible events that had deprived them of their livelihoods, families, property, and status, many still carried a deep attachment to Russia. Saddened by the political events and, at times, angry and bitter over what the Communists had done to them and their country, many lamented that their homeland had been closed off to them forever.

The Rise of Joseph Stalin

By 1924, Lenin, the leader of the Bolshevik revolution, was dead. In the wake of his death, a power struggle ensued among various factions of the Communist Party, who wrestled for control of the government. By 1929, Joseph Stalin had prevailed and imposed upon the country a reign of terror that lasted for more than twenty years. Under Stalin's leadership, what few freedoms had remained disappeared. The government tightened its control over almost every aspect of Soviet life, from where people could live to where they worked to when, where, and if they could travel.

Adding to the oppression and terror was a series of "purges" staged during the 1930s to cleanse the Communist Party and the state of its enemies. Fearful of being betrayed or deposed, Stalin attacked high-ranking officials, military leaders, and even ordinary citizens who were suspected, however vaguely, of disloyalty to

Life Under Stalin

For the majority of Russians, everyday life in the Soviet Union was difficult at best. At worst, it was unbearable. Everything was in short supply: food, clothing, even housing. Everything was the property of—and regulated by—the state. This fact made acquiring anything extremely difficult. Stalin believed that workers should earn their food based on how much work they did in a day. This meant that if a person did not work, he or she received an extremely small ration, usually no more than a thick slice of Russian bread. Even for those who did work, the daily allotment of food remained small and often pitifully inadequate. To complain about the lack of food, however, meant no food at all.

Clothing was also a problem. Under Stalin's regime, clothing and shoes were in great demand. Those that were available were poorly made, quickly fell apart, might have unevenly matched sleeves, or were missing buttons, pockets, collars, and the like.

Housing was another nightmare. The greatest problem was overcrowding, with numerous families living in apartments intended for a single family. If multiple families shared a living space, pots and pans became communal, as did most other household fixtures and appliances. Electricity and plumbing were often limited, if they existed at all. Stairways, hallways, and corridors were often filled with people who had no other housing. Residents and homeless people often used newspapers to keep warm or to cover holes in broken windows that they could not afford to have repaired.

Food, clothing, and housing were scarce under Joseph Stalin.

the government. These unfortunates often found themselves detained, tortured, and sent to one of the country's many labor camps, from which few ever returned.

Escapees, Not Émigrés

Despite Stalin's restrictions on travel, Russians continued to arrive in the United States after 1930, although they did so in decreasing numbers. Between 1930 and 1944, only 14,016 Russian immigrants entered the United States as compared to the millions who came during the nineteenth and early twentieth centuries. A number of factors were responsible for these smaller numbers. The Stalinist regime had made it virtually impossible for Soviet citizens to leave the country; those who did manage to leave were usually expelled from the country or left because they had to, often in fear for their lives.

The rise of Nazism in Germany during the 1930s and the Soviet Union's eventual entry into World War II also contributed to the smaller number of immigrants coming to the United States, because the chaos of wartime increased the risk involved in escaping the country. Prospective immigrants might be captured or killed by the enemy, or they might be stranded in an area where fighting was taking place. In June 1941, the German army invaded the Soviet Union and quickly overran the Russian countryside. Many Russians barely escaped German tanks entering their villages and cities. As the war dragged on, many Russians sought to escape the Nazi army, the air raids, and the battles fought where homes, churches, and farms had once stood. Thousands, bundling what they could carry, fled to the West.

A group of Russians emigrate from Stalin's restrictive Soviet Union.

The Second Wave: Russian Refugees

By the spring of 1945, World War II was over. Allied forces proved victorious in Europe, but the Soviet Union was a hulking, burning ruin. Yet there was an even greater problem facing the Allied forces: what to do with the approximately 8 million persons who had been displaced by the war, many of them refugees from the Soviet Union. Although many of the displaced people returned to the Soviet Union, it soon became apparent that a good number of them, approximately thirty-five thousand, did not want to return. The Soviet government, however, ordered these citizens home, stating that they did not have the right to decide where they wanted to live.

This situation put Allied officials in an awkward position. Before the refugees returned to Russia, all of the Allied powers, which included the United States, Great Britain, and the Soviet Union, had to agree on their eventual fate. Although the Allies at first agreed to send back Soviet citizens, after a few months the policy changed. With the exception of the Soviet Union, the Allies agreed to let the refugees decide where they wanted to live. By the end of 1945, official Allied policy stated that if a person disclaimed his or her Soviet citizenship, then he or she did not have to return to the Soviet Union. As difficult as it was to state that they were not citizens, many Soviets did so to avoid having to return to Stalinist Russia.

New Homes for New Residents

In solving one problem, however, the Allies created another: where to house the Soviet refugees. The American government stepped in with an offer to help by accepting the refugees who wished to come to the United States. Temporarily setting aside its restrictive immigration laws, the United States allowed the Soviet refugees free entry into the country. For the next four years, from July 1, 1947 until December 31, 1951 approximately 137,000 Soviet refugees entered the United States.

Unlike the Russian immigrants who came to the United States during the nineteenth and early twentieth centuries, the Soviet refugees who came after World War II had an easier time making the transition to American life. American officials arranged visits for them with representatives who asked about their education and abilities. As it turned out, many of the refugees had skills that the United States needed, ranging from skilled laborers to rocket scientists.

For those refugees who were teachers or physicians, though, finding a job was difficult. In order for them to continue in their chosen professions, they needed to learn English and then take an examination demonstrating that their abilities met American standards before they would be allowed to practice medicine or teach. Russian lawyers wishing to practice law in the United States found that they not only had to learn a new language but also had to understand American laws if they hoped to continue in their field.

All these challenges were made easier by the fact that the U.S. government assisted the refugees with the required medical examinations and also provided help in compiling the necessary travel documents such as passports, health certificates, and other important papers needed to enter the country. While waiting to leave for America, the refugees also attended English classes and learned about American life.

Once the newly arrived refugees entered the United States, officials helped them get to their new homes which were located around the country. This, too, was much different from the experiences of the previous generations. Whereas earlier immigrants tended to congregate in large cities, forming their own communities and neighborhoods, the refugees who came after World War II settled throughout the country in cities, towns, and rural areas. Initially, they suffered a great deal of loneliness and homesickness. One Russian doctor stated, "For you [Americans], it [Russia] is territory, but for me—it's my homeland."[29] However, in time many of the immigrants made themselves at home in their adopted country.

A New Kind of War

Having lost the battle to recover the refugees, the Stalinist government imposed even stricter emigration laws that severely limited the numbers of people allowed to leave the Soviet Union. The rationale for these restrictions ranged from fear of Western influence, which officials feared might incite political unrest in Russia, to preventing a mass exodus from the country. With Stalin still in power, it seemed that there was little that could be done for those wishing to leave.

Fear and distrust of the West, especially the United States, made even the mention of America or other Western countries a very dangerous proposition. Throughout Stalin's reign, people deemed enemies of the state were hauled off to labor camps or subjected to interrogation and torture by the Soviet secret police, the KGB. Some simply disappeared, never to be seen again. As one immigrant to the United States recalled:

Stalin's Daughter

One of the most infamous Russians to leave the Soviet Union was Svetlana Alliluyeva, the only daughter of Joseph Stalin; her defection in 1967 made international headlines. Born in 1926, Alliluyeva graduated from Moscow University, where she later taught Soviet literature and English. In 1965, she began working as a translator of Russian literature for a publishing house. The following year she was permitted to leave the Soviet Union to visit India. While there, she eluded officials at the Soviet Embassy and, with the help of American officials, defected to the United States in the spring of 1967. She burned her Soviet passport and became an American citizen in 1970. She also published two books: a memoir of her early life, *Twenty Letters to a Friend* (1967), and *Only One Year* (1969), which describes the events leading up to her defection and her reasons for doing so.

In 1984, Alliluyeva left the United States and returned to the Soviet Union, where despite her defection and criticisms of the Soviet government, she was welcomed and even had her Soviet citizenship restored. She also published her third book, *The Faraway Music* (1984). However, after clashing with Soviet authorities, probably over her criticisms of the government, she renounced her citizenship and moved back to the United States in 1986. She later moved once more, this time to England. Today she visits back and forth between the two countries.

Tolstoy Foundation

In 1939, Alexandra Tolstoy, the youngest daughter of Russian novelist Leo Tolstoy, founded the Tolstoy Foundation while she was living in New York City. Alexandra was one of the lucky few permitted to leave Soviet Russia in 1929 after being arrested five times and serving a prison sentence for supporting the right of free speech and assembly. She settled in the United States in 1931, where she engaged in farming and lectured widely in schools, universities, and clubs. She soon came to love her adopted country.

As president of the Tolstoy Foundation, Alexandra Tolstoy worked to build public support for international refugee relief efforts and to effect changes in U.S. immigration laws, as well as advocate human rights. Under her leadership, the foundation has helped more than 500,000 persons escape the horrors of war and political persecution in the Soviet Union and build new lives for themselves in America.

Alexandra Tolstoy helped thousands of Russians escape Soviet oppression.

Tolstoy also wanted to make sure that new immigrants assimilated quickly and successfully into American life without losing their cultural identities. To achieve this goal, the foundation, which moved to Reed Farm outside of New York City in 1941, has to date sponsored more than thirty thousand refugees. In some cases, if the refugees are elderly, they are allowed to stay at the farm for the rest of their lives. The foundation also provides training and work programs to help new immigrants adapt to life in America.

In 1950 we destroyed everything in the house that was linked to America. I put American magazines into the stove with all the letters from my Uncle Jacob [an American relative]. You could be jailed if you were found with one of those magazines. It meant that you were a propagandist of the American style of life and an enemy of the people.[30]

Upon Stalin's death in 1953, Nikita Khrushchev came to power, and throughout the Soviet Union many Russians hoped for a relaxation of the emigration laws. By this time, though, the Soviet Union and the United States were in the midst of what had become known as the cold war, a tense international standoff that lasted for nearly fifty years and made immigration to America difficult. The term *cold war* referred to an open yet restricted rivalry between the United States and the Soviet Union that was carried out through political and economic means and through the use of propaganda by both countries.

Behind the cold war rivalry were the two political systems of the Soviet Union and the United States. American democracy was in direct contradiction to the Soviet system of communism. Unlike in the United States, where the individual and individual rights were respected, almost every aspect of Soviet society was under the control of the government. As one former resident remembered:

Officially we are taught that we are all equal and that everybody is striving towards the communist goal. We are given to understand that the individual in the Soviet Union is nothing. We are taught that the Soviet people, all of them, want this, like this, hate that, don't need this. Every aspect of life is categorized and compartmentalized.[31]

The Third Wave: Dissidents and Exiles

Only during the late 1960s and early 1970s did the Soviet government institute a change of policy that allowed small numbers of citizens to leave the country. Two reasons accounted for the change. The first was the decisive victory by Israel over several of its Arab neighbors in the June 1967 conflict known as the Six-Day War. Not only did the Soviets support the Arab nations fighting Israel, they supplied them with weapons. As a result, many Russian Jews realized just how little regard the Soviet Union had for them. As one Jewish Russian later stated:

Until June 1967 Soviet Jews had illusions about co-existence with the regime, despite the fact that it [the Soviet government] wanted to destroy the Jewish state [Israel]. . . . [Then, in 1967,] Russia spat on the Jewish people and then we knew that we would never be able to live under such a regime.[32]

Second, as other countries put increasing pressure on the Soviet government to improve its treatment of the Jews and other citizens, Soviet leaders realized that to maintain the nation's position as a world power, its emigration policies had to change. Thus, during the early 1970s, as the Soviet Union and the United States signed a series of treaties intended to improve relations between the two countries, the Soviet government adopted a more tolerant attitude toward emigration, particularly Jewish emigration. These factors, then, ultimately contributed to an official change in policy. At last, many Russian Jews were given permission to join family members who had settled in Israel; others made the journey to America to be with family members who had settled there years earlier.

Besides the Russian Jews who received permission to leave, other Russians defected, or abandoned their country, when presented with an opportunity to leave. For many Russian artists, performers, scholars, and athletes, the opportunity to visit Western countries offered the chance to request political asylum without fear of being returned to the Soviet Union. For many of these individuals, living in the United States would allow them to pursue their art without constant input from the Soviet government.

In some cases, the defection of Russian artists proved to be dramatic. Mikhail Baryshnikov, for instance, a noted Russian ballet dancer, defected to the West in 1974 while performing with the Soviet Union's Bolshoi Ballet in Canada. Earlier, Baryshnikov had informed the U.S. government that he wished to defect to America. With the help of Jim Peterson, a Canadian government official, and John Fraser, a dance critic, plans were made to help Baryshnikov flee. Peterson later described the events of June 12, 1974, the evening that Baryishnikov defected after a ballet performance:

There was a crowd waiting and there was a number of cars waiting to take the company to a party afterwards. One of the people from the KGB said, "Misha [Baryshnikov], come and get in the car." Misha went towards the audience and said I have to sign some autographs and as soon as he got to the crowds, he bolted through it and ran three blocks up to the getaway car that was waiting. . . . I must confess that I was very frightened when we took the responsibility to organize this defection because . . . it was the heart of the Cold War. If we failed to get him away from the KGB that would be our last chance and if we were caught in the act then it could have been the last we ever saw of Baryshnikov.[33]

Baryshnikov later moved to New York City, where he established himself as one of the leading dancers in the world.

The 1970s also marked the emergence of a growing dissident movement in the Soviet Union. This dissatisfied portion of Soviet society was composed of a number of different protest groups, some of whom protested Soviet domination over the country's individual states (Russia, Ukraine, etc.); others protested the government's treatment of the Jews. Branded in the Soviet Union as "undesirables," this group included many writers, artists, musicians, and scientists who were critical of Communist ideology and life under the Soviet dictatorship. The dissenters had little trouble receiving permission to come to the United States; in fact, the Soviet government often forced them to leave, and the Americans welcomed people who fought communism.

The Closing of the Gates

By 1985, though, the gates to freedom had closed once more to Soviet citizens. An invasion of the small central Asian country of Afghanistan by Soviet forces in 1979 intensified the cold war, worsening relations between the Soviet Union and the United States again. The United States cut back on cultural and trade agreements and placed an embargo, or boycott, on its shipping of grain to the Soviet Union. In response, the Soviet Union cut back on emigration from the

Russian ballet dancer Mikhail Baryshnikov defected to the West in 1974 while performing in Canada with the Bolshoi Ballet.

A Writer Returns Home

Novelist Alexander Solzhenitsyn remains one of the most famous of all Russian political dissidents and exiles. His problems with the Soviet government first began in 1945 when he was arrested for writing a letter in which he criticized Joseph Stalin. He spent the next eight years in prisons and labor camps, after which he spent three more years living as an outcast in Soviet society. In 1956, Solzhenitsyn again began writing. Encouraged by the loosening of government restraints on cultural life during the early 1960s, Solzhenitsyn submitted his short novel *One Day in the Life of Ivan Denisovich* to a leading Soviet literary magazine. The novel enjoyed immediate popularity, but the story, which describes a typical day in the life of an inmate of a labor camp during the Stalin era, also brought sharp criticism from the Soviet government. Solzhenitsyn found himself harassed by state authorities as his criticisms of the repressive Soviet policies mounted. By 1963, he was prohibited from publishing his work, and he resorted to circulating it secretly and having it smuggled out of the country to be published abroad. In 1970 Solzhenitsyn was awarded the Nobel Prize for literature, but he declined to attend the ceremony in Stockholm, Sweden, fearing that the government, which had at first denied him permission to go, would not let him reenter Russia if he left the country.

Upon publication of the first volume of *The Gulag Archipelago* in 1973, which documents Solzhenitsyn's own experiences in the Stalinist labor camps, he was attacked in the Soviet press. A year later, despite the intense interest in his fate by the West, Solzhenitsyn was arrested by the Soviet government and charged with treason. He was exiled from the Soviet Union the following day. Later, he came to the United States and settled in Vermont.

With the adoption of the new Soviet policy of glasnost, or "openness," during the late 1980s, in which the Soviet Union began, among other things, relaxing its ban on certain types of literature, Solzhenitsyn's work once more became available in that country. In 1990, Solzhenitsyn's Soviet citizenship was officially restored; four years later, the author returned home.

Novelist Alexander Solzhenitsyn was exiled for speaking out against Stalin and the Soviet government.

country. Jewish emigration in particular fell by more than 60 percent in 1980, and between 1983 and 1986, the average number of Soviets allowed to leave was approximately one thousand; a decade earlier, the number had been more than twenty-five thousand.

Many Russians who had come to America as part of the three waves of immigration watched carefully as the political climate changed again between the United States and their homeland. For many, it was a painful reminder of how quickly events—whether a revolution, a war, or a change in government—can change one's life and how those changes had brought many of them to a new home in America.

CHAPTER FOUR

Becoming American

Whether fleeing the czar or the Communists, the newly arrived Russians faced a host of new challenges. Many came to America with no contacts or family. Few could speak English, even fewer had jobs, and many had less than $50 in their pockets. Yet somehow, despite the difficulties with language, housing, and employment, the Russians managed to adapt to life in the United States. In the process, they created communities that enabled them not only to learn about America but also to keep intact many of the customs, values, and institutions they had left behind in Russia.

Once they arrived in the United States, the Russian immigrants fanned out. Al-though statistics show that the immigrants clustered primarily along the northeast and Atlantic seaboard, with the greatest number settling in New York, some settled in Illinois, Maryland, Ohio, North Dakota, Texas, and Washington. Still others traveled farther west to California and even Hawaii.

The "Black Work"

Because the majority of Russians who immigrated to the United States could not speak English and often lacked professional skills, the jobs available to them usually involved manual labor. Russians who settled in New York state and Pennsylvania, for instance, went to work in the coal mines or in one of the many steel factories located in these areas. Others who settled in Chicago or elsewhere in the Midwest found work in the slaughterhouses and meat-packing plants. Some Russian immigrants, especially Russian Jews, found employment as seamstresses, tailors, pressers, and cutters in factories and sweatshops that manufactured clothing. Russians also found work in canneries, on the railroads, in the sugar beet factories, or in logging camps. No matter what the job, the immigrants called it "black work," which referred to the dirty and menial nature of the task. One woman who came to New York from Russia in 1895 went to work in a garment sweatshop. She described the harsh working conditions she found there:

> We sat in long rows, our bodies bent over the machines, the work we turned out fell into wooden bins attached to the part of the machine facing us. No one girl made an entire garment. As each girl completed her part the garment was passed on to the next girl by Levinson [the foreman] who was always walking back and forth urging us on. Should a girl lag behind he would prod her, sometimes pulling on the garment to hurry it on to another worker. . . . This sort of thing created a spirit of competition for self preservation that ended only when the worker, too weak to compete longer with a stronger sister, broke down.[34]

All of these jobs demanded long hours for very low wages. In 1909, for example, the average daily pay for a Russian laborer was $2.06, or approximately 17 cents an hour for a twelve-hour workday. (During World War I, wages did increase; some workers earned an average of $23 a week.) During the 1920s, studies showed that Russian immigrant steel workers labored twelve hours a day, seven days a week. Every two weeks, they were required to work an eighteen- or twenty-four-hour day when adjusting from the day to the night shift.

Working long hours was bad enough, but often the jobs Russian immigrants performed were among the most dangerous. For instance, in the steel mills one of the worst jobs involved conditioning molten steel. Men lifted large paper sacks filled with coal and then carried them to a huge iron ladle filled with white-hot molten steel. Next, they threw the coal sacks into

Russians who arrived in America often worked long hours in the steel mills.

the ladle, causing the steel to flame up. Careless or tired workers performing this job stood a good chance of being burned or losing their balance and slipping into the ladle.

Another job in the steel mill often reserved for Russian immigrant workers was in the checker chamber room attached to an open hearth, or furnace. The checker chamber contained red-hot bricks that were used to draw and heat the air for the furnace. In order to make sure the furnace stayed hot, the bricks were changed on a regular basis by workers inside the checker chamber. One observer noted that he could not have stayed more than ten minutes in the room, the heat was so intense. Scientists even stated that the room temperature was so hot that it would have been impossible for life to sustain itself. Yet factory owners continued to send Russian workers into the rooms, where they worked in thirty-minute shifts removing and replacing the bricks.

Dangers and Discrimination

Despite the dangerous conditions that many Russian immigrants faced at their jobs, factory owners and foremen did little in the way of protecting them. If a worker was injured on the job, he had virtually no recourse; few companies offered medical or disability benefits. The inability to speak English also prevented Russian immigrants from applying for what forms of workmen's compensation did exist. Factories and companies were also notorious for concealing from their workers any money owed to them as a result of job-related injuries. Harry Germanow, who came to the United States from Russia in 1909, recalled his experience with an on-the-job injury he suffered at the Crane shipyards in Philadelphia:

> One morning about 10 o'clock, I met with an accident. Working on a drill press trying to change a belt from a slow speed to a faster one, my second finger of my right hand caught in open gears and chopped a piece of my finger off. In those days machines were not guarded [had no safety shields] as [they are] now. There were no labor inspectors. I was taken to a hospital where my finger was trimmed and bandaged. I was paid for the day's work till 10 o'clock only.[35]

In addition to unsafe working conditions, Russian immigrants also endured discrimination at the hands of their employers. It was common for the boss or foreman at a factory or mine to shout insults at Russian workers. One worker recalled that his boss was "worse than the Tsar's officials; they would flog [hit] us and let us go, he drives us to a slow death."[36] Some Russian immigrants complained of being docked a portion of their pay for being a minute late to work; others told of men being fired on the spot for leaving to get a drink of water. One worker aptly summed up the general treatment Russian immigrants received, saying that the bosses "treat Russians like a dog."[37]

Many Russian immigrants also faced discrimination because of their supposed political affiliations, especially if they were

The Russian Press

Next to the Orthodox Church, the greatest influences in the Russian immigrant community were the Russian-language newspapers. By the beginning of the twentieth century, a number of Russian-language newspapers were being published throughout the United States, the majority in New York City and Chicago. They reached their zenith in the 1920s. Some of these papers were the first radical and socialist newspapers to appear in the United States. They gave many Americans a glimpse of the political philosophies that toppled the czarist regime and precipitated political unrest in many other European nations.

The frequency with which the newspapers were published and the information included in them varied. Some appeared as monthlies and others weekly. Some were strictly political in outlook, while others combined humor or current events. Russian-language newspapers that published daily editions carried national and international news as well as local events and advertisements. Many papers, through their "Letters to the Editor" section, also provided an outlet for readers, allowing immigrants to voice their opinions about the United States, Russia, and any number of other topics.

Today, only one Russian American newspaper has survived. The *Novoe russkoe slovo* ("New Russian World") began publishing in New York City in 1910 and is considered the world's oldest Russian-language newspaper. Its yearly circulation is approximately forty-three thousand, with the majority of the paper's readership made up of Russian immigrants who arrived during the 1960s and '70s.

Russian-language newspapers were a great influence in the Russian-American community.

suspected of belonging to the Communist Party. At numerous companies, Russians were laid off or fired as soon as their employers found out they were Russian. One former YMCA (Young Men's Christian Association) employee who worked with many Russian immigrants recalled:

Since the "Bolshevik" [Communist] regime began in Russia, the Russian is regarded everywhere as a "Bolshevik" and is shunned. I encountered a case the other day where an employer got the idea that the distinguishing feature of a "Bolshevik" was a beard, so he refused to give employment to some faithful and loyal Old Believers [a Russian Orthodox religious group] whose religious conviction does not permit them to shave. Whenever the employer has found it necessary to cut down the number of employees the Russian has been the first to go.[38]

These prejudices further isolated many Russian immigrants from the American mainstream. In response, some Russian immigrants refused to have much to do with becoming American. Some refused to learn English, while others criticized American ways. As one observer put it, "He [the Russian immigrant] begins to hate America and everything American, and is ready to believe anything bad about her."[39]

Russian immigrants faced difficulties outside of the workplace too. Those wishing to buy land might be cheated by land agents who sold them property that was impossible to farm. Private banks took advantage of the immigrants by taking their money and then pretending to go bankrupt, making it impossible for immigrants to retrieve their funds. Doctors of disreputable skill often took immigrants on as their patients, overcharging them for treatment and then failing to provide them with adequate medical care. Shopkeepers and grocers were also known to take advantage of Russian immigrants' lack of English by overcharging them or cheating them on the price of goods.

Their Own Boss

As a result of the poor working conditions, low wages, and prejudice, some Russian immigrants, many of them Jewish, decided to open their own businesses. Many men started out as peddlers, salesmen who went from street to street or door to door selling everything from pots and pans to buttons, needles, and cloth. Peddling was hard work, as Henry Seessel, who moved to New Orleans, Louisiana, remembered: "I did not relish the idea of peddling at all. Everytime we stopped . . . to sell goods I had to pack the heavy packages in and out of the houses."[40] The hard work sometimes paid off. If they were enterprising peddlers could make as much as $500 in two weeks.

Many Russian Jews who owned their own stores provided specialized goods and services to the community; kosher butchers are one example. Others tended to everyday needs, running small grocery stores. Here, neighborhood residents could stop in to buy a loaf of bread, some potatoes, wood for the stove, and penny candy for a special treat for their children. Other immigrants worked as shoe-shine boys or delivery drivers. Immigrants with specialized skills might also go into business for themselves; for example, one immigrant in Rhode Island made stone carvings and metal decorations for the exteriors of buildings.

Russian Immigrants and the Labor Unions

Although owning one's own business was sometimes a lucrative way to make money, the majority of Russian laborers worked for large companies, factories, or mills. As a result of the poor treatment they received in these workplaces, Russian immigrants were among the most ardent supporters of the American labor, or workers, movement. Numbering in the thousands, they were active in all aspects of labor-organizing activity, from participating in strikes to helping raise awareness among workers about issues such as better pay and safer working conditions. Although most Russians could not join American trade unions, labor unions for skilled workers only, many did join the groups that were open to all workers, including the United Mine Workers of America and the radical International Workers of the World. There was even a union exclusively for Russians known as the Union of Russian Workers.

Some Russians, though, viewed the unions, like many other things American, with suspicion and dis-

dain. They had come to resent the treatment they received in the United States, and often viewed all Americans as potential enemies who were scheming to take advantage of them in some way. One Russian woman told an interviewer, "We know now that America means money. We Russians are like flies, too small—company doesn't care."[41]

At Home

Even in their homes, Russian immigrants continued to experience a growing sense of

Police respond to a nineteenth-century Pennsylvania labor strike. Russian immigrants were often ardent supporters of the American labor movement.

isolation in their new country. Like other immigrant groups such as the Italians and the Chinese, the Russians created their own communities, often in neighborhoods that others had earlier settled and later abandoned. Although these communities lent themselves to keeping distinct traditions and institutions intact, they also in some ways hindered the Russian immigrants' progress in assimilating to American life. Provided with everything they needed, including food, social activities, and a church, Russian immigrants were less inclined to leave their neighborhoods, except to go to work.

In these neighborhoods, home for many Russians during the late nineteenth and

A young girl chops wood in front of a New York tenement. After arriving in America, many Russians settled in overcrowded tenement buildings.

early twentieth centuries was an apartment in an overcrowded tenement building. A study done in 1911 estimated that 2.85 persons lived in a single sleeping room in most Russian homes. Another study done in 1919 showed that, in a Chicago tenement building with thirty apartments, an average of 7.2 Russian immigrants lived in a four-room apartment. Overcrowding was nothing new to the Russians: Many had lived with similar conditions in their own country. Thus, most did not see living with many people under one roof as a hardship.

Conditions in many of these buildings, however, were terrible. Most apartments had only one window, and toilet facilities were shared by anywhere from eight to nineteen persons. Some apartments might have a bathtub, but residents usually used it more often for doing the laundry than for bathing. One journalist visiting Manhattan's Lower East Side, where many Russian Jews lived, described in an 1888 article what he found in the tenements he visited:

> They are great prison-like structures of brick, with narrow doors and windows, cramped passages and steep rickety stairs. . . . The narrow courtyard . . . in the middle is a damp, foul smelling place, supposed to do double duty as an air shaft. . . . They could not have been more villainously arranged to avoid any chance of ventilation. . . . In case of fire they would be perfect deathtraps, for it would be impossible for the occupants of the crowded rooms to escape by the narrow stairways[,] and flimsy fire escapes . . . are

so laden with broken furniture, bales, and boxes that they would be worse than useless.[42]

Living conditions in the mining communities were just as bad, if not worse. One researcher visiting a Russian mining community in Pennsylvania described the filthy conditions he encountered:

> The coal and iron mining regions of the country . . . show some of our worst housing conditions. Shacks are built by individuals and by mining companies close to mine shafts [and] pits. Tin cans, tar paper, and old boards furnish building materials for crazy shelters. Into one or more small rooms crowd the large families of the workmen. Toilets are either absent, or else miserable privies are erected and neglected. Outdoor pumps furnish water, and the ground surface serves as a sewer.[43]

Many Russian immigrants in the mining towns boarded in homes either owned or rented by other Russian immigrants. Staying in places like these, the Russians were assured of being able to speak their own language and talk about things that were common to almost everyone else around them. It also guaranteed that meals would include at least one or two foods that many had grown up with. Although these and other establishments were comforting and provided some measure of security to the immigrants, they also made it less likely that they would try to learn American ways.

A Helping Hand

One of the most interesting Russian immigrant social organizations was the Mutual Aid for Russian Workers. The group's purpose was to provide a variety of services for immigrants arriving or already settled in the city of Boston. Groups like these were invaluable for new immigrants: They provided a friendly face, a familiar language, and desperately needed advice and reassurance about life in America.

Within each group, a member was designated an "expert" on some particular need. One member, for instance, might know everything about buying steamship tickets to come to America, while another knew where the best jobs could be found. Someone else knew all about housing, while another person investigated the ways to send money to relatives in Russia. Each of the experts was a volunteer, and the group made sure that no one profited from secret arrangements with a shipping company, employer, or landlord.

A nurse watches over a group of small children. Mutual Aid societies helped immigrants with a variety of services, including finding housing and jobs.

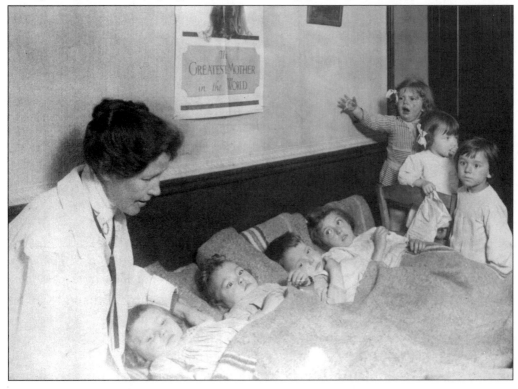

"I'm an Americanka"

Although many Russian immigrants shunned American ways, there were plenty of others eager to adapt to their new homeland. To learn as much as they could about the United States and becoming an American citizen, large numbers of Russian immigrants attended English classes, enrolled their children in public schools, and took advantage of the services offered by social organizations such as the YMCA. Russian Jews were particularly willing to leave behind Russian ways. Instead, they concentrated on establishing a culture in which they could practice their religion and way of life without fear.

An immigrant's introduction to American culture could be quite humorous. In 1892, for instance, thirteen-year-old Mary Antin came to the United States from Russia. Her first view of her new home in Boston and its surroundings offered many memorable experiences. She wrote:

Many Russian immigrants, like this New Jersey woman, embraced life in their new home.

The first meal was an object lesson of much variety. My father produced several kinds of food, ready to eat, without any cooking, from little tin cans that had printing all over them. He attempted to introduce us to a queer slippery kind of fruit, which he called "banana," but had to give it up for the time being. After the meal, he had better luck with a curious piece of furniture on runners, which he called "rocking chair."[44]

For many immigrants, learning to speak English was one of the greatest challenges, and in some homes Russian families spoke English at all times in an effort to master the language. Speaking English was not only a sign that one was becoming American; for many Russian immigrants, it was also a source of pride. For Sonia Walinsky, who came from Russia in 1906, learning to speak a few words of English was one of the greatest moments of her life. She later told an interviewer, "When people spoke to me in Russian, I said 'Speak only English. I'm an Americanka now. Don't speak Russian to me. I'm an Americanka.'"[45]

Family Life

Although the majority of the first Russian immigrants were single, many families also immigrated to the United States. In most cases, the husband and father was the head

A Place Like Home

Prior to World War II, Russia was still largely an agricultural nation. As a result, some Russian immigrants arriving in America established their own rural communities much like the small villages and towns they grew up in. For instance, during the 1930s, Russian immigrants who had grown up in the Don Cossack region of Russia (an area located along the lower Don River) started a number of farming communities in southern New Jersey such as Lakewood, Cassville, and Howell, which are still around today.

Other Russian immigrants who could afford to do so rented weekend houses in rural areas. These weekend retreats to the country had a high price. Because most Russians worked on Saturdays and Sundays, they often had to take as many as three trains back to the city to reach their jobs. Often this meant getting up as early as four in the morning and not returning until after ten at night. But for those who could do it, the effort was well worth the trouble. Spending weekends in the country afforded them and their families fresh air and open space. For many Russians, the opportunity to enjoy country living was the chance of a lifetime.

---

of the household and the main source of income. Many Russian wives and mothers stayed at home, but they also helped with the family finances by taking in boarders and doing sewing, laundry, or other types of piecework. In some cases, the husband worked at night, while the wife found a day job.

For the women of the house, days were long and hard. Up early in the morning, Russian women had their families to look after and, if they had boarders, they saw to their meals and laundry as well. For some women, this meant taking care of more than twenty persons every single day. In addition, women did the shopping, mending, or any other work as needed. These chores left many Russian women exhausted at the end of the day, with little time for leisure activity.

Immigrant Kids

For children, coming to America was filled with both exciting and frightening experiences. For the first time, many children were enrolled in public schools and had an opportunity to get an education. Often, the children attended classes until they were old enough to work, usually at the age of fourteen when they could obtain full-time working papers, but it was not unheard of for children to begin working earlier, especially if the family needed money.

In many households, children were often the first to learn English and were also the first to pick up on American customs, including current trends in fashions, manners, and speech. Children then often acted as translators for their parents or other adults in the household when it came time to read anything in English, whether important documents or the newspaper.

Still, the transition between the old and the new was not without conflict. Many Russian immigrant households struggled between the old Russian ways of the parents and the new American customs that the children adopted. Some parents feared the loss of their heritage and their history as their children adopted more and more American ways. Yet seeing their children adapting to American society also represented the possibility of Russian immigrant families making a life for themselves in their new home.

Rita Seitzer, who came to the United States as a young girl, remembered vividly her mother's heartache at the changes American life brought to the family:

> My mother did not learn English. She never adjusted. She was an old-fashioned woman. . . . It hurt her to see her children not observe the old ways, but she never said anything. I know she was hurt, but she didn't try to change us. . . . Maybe she realized that we were living in a different country, and we can't be the same as we were at home.[46]

A Russian Way of Worship

The Russian immigrants may have come to America with very little in their pockets, but they did not come completely empty-handed. Like the members of many other immigrant groups, the Russians established their own institutions, including churches, social groups, and clubs that not only

helped them hold on to their identity but also aided with the sometimes painful transition to life in the United States.

From the outset, the Russian Orthodox Church was always closely associated with Russian immigration; its establishment in North America dates from the settlement of the Alaskan colonies. As each new group of Russian immigrants came and settled in

Parishioners enter an orthodox church in New Jersey. The Russian Orthodox Church was an essential part of immigrants' lives.

America, the church grew, eventually becoming the largest and most powerful Orthodox denomination in America.

During the early years of the twentieth century, Russian immigrants also built 126 Orthodox schools throughout the United States. These schools provided instruction in Orthodox theology, church history, and Russian history for children. All classes were taught in Russian as a way of making sure that the children remained connected to their heritage and their community. In addition to the schools, the Orthodox Church built a girl's college, seminaries in Minnesota and New Jersey, a monastery in Pennsylvania, a home for immigrants, and an orphanage. The church also sponsored the Russia Orthodoxy of Mutual Aid, which provided assistance and guidance to Russian immigrants.

Dissenting Opinions

Although the Orthodox Church offered spiritual and material comfort for many Russians, there were still problems. As the state church of Russia, the Orthodox Church strongly supported the czar and expected worshipers to do the same. Many Russian immigrants, though, had come to the United States to get away from the czar, not to continue to pay tribute to him. Some churchgoers resented having to give money to the church because they knew that a portion of it was sent back to Russia as a show of allegiance to the czar. Many immigrants were also angry that each parish had to follow the dictates of a central church authority instead of being able to make decisions, such as the naming of priests, on their own.

By the time of the Bolshevik revolution in 1917, many Russian immigrants had become angry and dissatisfied with the way church officials in America treated them. As a result, attendance at church services declined, with members coming only to special services on holidays. From that point on, the Orthodox Church, although remaining an important element in the Russian immigrant community even today, never commanded the absolute obedience that it once enjoyed.

Honoring the Sabbath

One of the hopes for the thousands of Russian Jews who came to America was to live in a country that allowed religious freedom. Upon arriving in the United States, they immediately took advantage of that opportunity. Everywhere they settled, they organized synagogues where members of the community could worship and Hebrew schools where Jewish children learned to speak Hebrew, the traditional Jewish language, and learned about their religion's history. Hilda Malkin, the daughter of immigrants, attended Hebrew school from the time she was six until she was twelve. She recalled that "Hebrew school was very important. I had to learn to read Hebrew, to pray . . . so that when I grew up I would be able to pass this heritage on."[47]

One of the most important traditions in the Russian Jewish community was the observance of the Sabbath. No matter where they lived, all Russian Jews observed the same ritual every week. According to historians:

At sundown on Friday, when the Sabbath begins, the shops of the Jewish

Making Do

U pon moving to the United States, Russian immigrants often found themselves having to make do with poor living conditions and food choices. In America, the immigrants usually bought their food at a neighborhood grocery store, where the selection was limited and prices high. Quality, too, was a problem; often the food was old, stale, or spoiled. One item that many Russians could afford, for example, was poor cuts of meat. These meats were often heavy in fat and gristle and sometimes infected by harmful bacteria. As Russians added these meats to their diets, they increased the risk of contracting diseases or suffering from ongoing digestive troubles.

The immigrants' living conditions were also breeding grounds for infectious diseases; tuberculosis, for instance, was a frequent visitor to many Russian immigrant homes. However, the Russians tended to make little use of the health facilities that were available to them. Children were usually born at home with the help of a midwife, and home remedies were more commonly used than prescription medicines. For many, the main stumbling block to U.S. health care was a lack of knowledge of English, but others admitted that they simply did not trust American doctors.

American neighborhoods closed. In traditional Jewish households, the men go to synagogue for Sabbath evening service, while at home mothers prepare for the Sabbath dinner. Because cooking is forbidden on the Sabbath, meals are cooked before sundown. As the mother of the family recites a blessing, she lights candles to illuminate the house during the Sabbath.[48]

Observing the Sabbath and other religious holidays were family affairs. Relatives got together to celebrate. In this way, the Jewish religion not only promoted worship but encouraged strong family ties.

Being with Their Own Kind

Family bonds proved crucial to the assimilation of all Russian immigrants, Jewish or not. Such strong beliefs in family and community allowed the Russians a means of maintaining and expressing their own cultural traditions. The immigrants often congregated in their neighborhoods, forming social groups or cultural organizations that allowed them to be with other people whose experiences were similar to their own. One of the mainstays for Russian immigrants during the late nineteenth and early twentieth centuries were social clubs. These clubs were important to the community because they not only served as a place for Russian immigrants to meet and talk but were in many instances a

Dressing the Part

For some new Russian arrivals, buying American clothing for the first time was one of the most memorable experiences they had. Sophie Abrams, who came to New York City in 1920, remembers her first shopping trip. Dorothy and Thomas Hoobler quote Abrams in their book The Jewish American Family Album.

My first day in America I went with my aunt to buy some American clothes. She bought me a shirtwaist, you know, a blouse and a skirt, a blue print with red buttons and a hat, such a hat, I had never seen. I took my old brown dress and shawl and threw them away! I know it sounds foolish, we being so poor, but I didn't care. I had enough of the old country. When I looked in the mirror, I couldn't get over it. I said, boy, Sophie, look at you now. Just like an American.

clearinghouse for information and advice on how to live successfully in America. In addition, these organizations might offer special services to the Russian immigrants such as burial insurance, mutual aid policies for widows and children, and insurance policies to cover accidents and illness.

Cultural enrichment organizations were also popular. One of the largest was *Nauka* (which is the Russian word for science). Organized in 1905, *Nauka* offered death benefits and insurance, as did many other mutual aid societies, but it also sponsored reading rooms, concerts, lectures, and socials. Other groups such as *Znamenie* (the Sign), *Samo Obrazovanie* (the Society of Self-Education), *Prosvishenie* (Enlightenment), and the Society of Russian Citizens offered similar services and social opportunities.

A number of organizations also formed in response to the political uncertainties in Russia and later the Soviet Union. In Los Angeles, for instance, the Society to Help Free Russia was created to help people emigrate from Russia, and other groups arose to help those who wished to return. Although these groups and others like them were certainly intended to offer immigrants financial or political assistance, they were usually very small and had limited financial resources. Thus, the groups were often just used as an excuse to gather socially.

Although Russian Jews sometimes joined these Russian clubs, particularly those sponsored by labor unions, they had their own organizations as well. The Workmen's Circle, for instance, was an organization of laborers offering help to those who could not find work. There were also Jewish mutual aid societies, known as *landmanshaften,* made up of Russian Jews who all came from the same area of Russia. These groups offered insurance and interest-free loans and helped care for the elderly and the sick members of the Jewish community.

Learning to adjust, whether by forming community organizations or speaking English, was undoubtedly the key to success for many Russian immigrants. And although some immigrants resisted being pulled into the mainstream of American culture, most Russian Americans enjoyed the personal freedom life in the United States offered while still keeping traditions alive.

CHAPTER FIVE

Differences Within and Without

Almost all immigrant groups faced discrimination and prejudice when they came to the United States. For Russian immigrants, however, these biases were intensified by the rivalry of the cold war. Americans often regarded Russian immigrants as members of the Communist Party, or at least sympathetic to the Communist philosophy, despite the fact that many had fled to the United States to escape Communist oppression and terror.

Following the collapse of the Soviet Union in 1991, American relations with Russia improved. And while most Russian immigrants today are not regarded with the same suspicion as those who came even a

decade before them, many Russians still face the same obstacles as earlier generations. In general, today's immigrants are intellectually better prepared to come to America; most of them know quite a bit about the United States and its culture. But still, new immigrants find themselves harboring feelings of awkwardness, uncertainty, and sometimes anger toward their new home.

Comrades or Compatriots?

As the drama of the Bolshevik revolution unfolded between 1917 and 1921, Russian immigrants to the United States followed each development closely. For many, their reason for leaving Russia in the first place had been the oppressive czarist regime, which was now no longer in power. Although most Russian immigrants did not completely understand the political developments that had taken place in their country, they did know that the new government was calling itself a "workers' state," leaving many immigrants hopeful that at last the common people of Russia would have a say in how they lived. The triumph of communism in Russia, the immigrants believed, suggested the beginning of a utopian future that promised greater equality, democracy, and prosperity than anywhere else in the world, including the United States.

The events in the Soviet Union caused many Russian immigrants to consider returning home. These sentiments grew even stronger when the U.S. government made clear its disapproval of the new Communist regime, refusing to recognize the new government's legitimacy. For most Americans, Communist ideology stood in direct and startling opposition to the principles of political and economic freedom that the United States represented. The two systems of government and society were simply irreconcilable.

Between 1917 and 1920, the U.S. government denied permission to those Russians who wished to go home. Many Russian immigrants protested against this policy, arguing that the U.S. government was fostering the same kinds of restrictions the czarist government had imposed. Following World War I, as these immigrants pressed harder for permission to leave the country, a fear of communism swept the United States. Known as the "Red Scare," it had important implications for both Americans and Russian immigrants.

The Red Scare

In the weeks leading up to the end of World War I, the U.S. Congress passed a

A 1919 political cartoon depicts U.S. fears that communism threatened the American way of life.

new law known as the Sedition Act. Under this provision, the government called for "the exclusion and expulsion of all United States aliens who are members of anarchist and similar classes."[49] In effect, this law made it possible for government authorities to deport aliens whose political beliefs or affiliations made them suspect, even if they had committed no crime. The law was the product of a growing fear of communism in America, specifically the concern that the Bolshevik revolution would spread to the United States.

Tensions ran high in the United States during the early 1920s. In addition to the perceived Communist threat, rising unemployment, a higher cost of living, a shortage of housing, and falling farm prices put the American people on edge. Race riots in twenty-six American cities in 1919 and the increased militancy of organized labor only added to the anxiety.

It did not help that many Russians closely associated themselves with the labor movement, which was considered by many Americans to be a hotbed of communism. Russian immigrants' participation in radical political parties that sometimes resorted to terrorism also hardened American attitudes toward Russian immigrants. Many Americans viewed them as socialists, anarchists, or Communists (all of whose political beliefs called for the overthrow of the American government), and they were deemed "un-American." When a series of bombings occurred during several labor strikes in cities throughout the nation, the federal government decided to act before the labor unrest got out of hand.

Attorney General A. Mitchell Palmer, whose own home had been bombed, sought to put an end to the terrorist attacks. Palmer called for police raids on suspicious organizations, particularly those in which Russian immigrants were known to participate. In this way, Palmer hoped to put an end to any kind of seditious activity in the United States.

Raids and Deportation

In February 1919, as part of Palmer's plan to stop Communist activities in the United States, New York police raided the headquarters of the Union of Russian Peasant Workers of America, arresting several hundred men and women. On New Year's Day 1920, a similar raid was conducted against

Attorney General A. Mitchell Palmer was determined to stop Communist activity in the United States.

The "Soviet Ark"

One of the most horrible acts sanctioned by the American government during the Red Scare came toward the end of A. Mitchell Palmer's quest to rid the United States of "undesirables." At midnight on Saturday, December 20, 1919, 249 immigrants detained at Ellis Island as a result of the Palmer raids were told to move from their quarters. The order came so quickly that many did not even have a chance to gather what few possessions they had brought with them. Some were still awaiting reviews of their cases, while others were expecting to be released on bail. Instead, they were lined up and marched under armed guard to a ferry. From there they were transferred to the *Buford,* an army transport ship waiting to take them back across the Atlantic. The ship took the group to Finland, where they then boarded a train full of armed guards, which transported them to the Soviet border and simply left them there.

Scattered among the group of anarchists and labor radicals were a number of men who left families behind and a few teenage girls whose families could not afford to help them. Many of the group had come to the United States as infants or small children and had no memory of life in Russia.

---

the headquarters of the American Communist Party in New York City. In fact, during a sixteen-month period between 1919 and 1920, as police raided union organizations in search of weapons and explosives, approximately sixty-five hundred persons were arrested for alleged violations of the Sedition Act. Of this number, about five hundred Russians who were not American citizens were sent to Ellis Island to await deportation to the Soviet Union. Of the purported large caches of weapons and explosives that had served as a pretext for many of the raids, the police netted a total of three pistols.

Because Russians were often the primary targets of suspicion and of Palmer's raids, approximately 90 percent of those detained were sent back to the Soviet Union, although many were, in fact, hostile to the new Communist government. None of the suspects got a chance to defend themselves in court. All were immediately judged guilty without trial largely because of their nationality. Even Ellis Island, once viewed as the gateway to a new life in America, was now routinely called the "Socialist Hall" and was seen as a breeding ground for what one observer called "Red revolutionaries . . . a club where Europe's offscourings [outcasts] are entertained at American expense."[50]

As a result of the Red Scare, anyone who was of Russian descent, whether Communist or anti-Communist, became the target of a government investigation. The consequences were that hundreds of Russian immigrants lost their jobs and their homes simply because they were Russian.

Some immigrants tried to blend in more with American society by converting to Protestantism or changing their names in the hope that their true identities would remain undetected by police and government authorities; sometimes this worked, and sometimes it did not. Regardless, by the spring of 1920 the Red Scare had passed. Yet the attitudes it fostered toward the Russian immigrant community never completely disappeared.

Deciphering the Differences

Russian immigrants also faced divisiveness within their own community. These divisions became more pronounced after the Bolshevik revolution, when many "White" Russians (those who had opposed the Communists and, in some cases, supported the czar) came to the United States. These immigrants, on the whole, received a friendlier welcome in the United States, in large part because their political sympathies were similar to those of many Americans. Furthermore, because they were generally better educated and perhaps more eager to learn American ways, the White Russians often adapted more easily to life in America than the immigrants who had arrived before them.

The belief that this group of immigrants was receiving better treatment because of their political sympathies generated resentment within the Russian immigrant community. Those who had arrived before World War I accused the White Russian immigrants of trying to take over or replace the organizations they had struggled to build and maintain. Working-class immigrants also took offense at the apparent ease with which the newcomers assimilated into American society. For their part, the White Russians could not understand how their fellow immigrants could show so little concern for what was happening to the mother country, or worse, could support the new Communist regime.

New Arrivals, Old Problems

Similar attitudes also greeted Russian immigrants who began arriving in America during the 1970s. By then, they no longer made the journey in the sweltering confines of a steerage cabin but by jet plane. The trip was generally a flight from Moscow to New York City, with a layover perhaps in Rome, Vienna, or London. Older immigrants viewed the new arrivals as not worthy of the hardships they had endured. To them, arriving in America by plane with many of their possessions was not the same as fleeing the swords of the Cossacks, the guns of the Nazis, the long arm of the czar and his secret police, or the Communists. Older immigrants also thought that these newer immigrants did not flee for their lives in coming to the United States but came instead with the hope of making money, in order to buy expensive clothes, big-screen television sets, fancy cars, and lavish homes.

These complaints notwithstanding, the new wave of Russian immigrants faced a distinct set of problems. Although many of the hardships they endured were bureaucratic in nature, they still made for a difficult, and at times frightening, transition to a new life in America.

"Nonpersons"

The first obstacle new immigrants wrestled with was travel itself. Under the Soviet government, ordinary Russians did not enjoy the right to come and go freely. The only people who could go abroad were representatives of the government, performers, and athletes, and only then under strict supervision. For immigrants coming to the United States since the 1970s, getting permission to leave was nothing short of a miracle. To leave the Soviet Union, a person first applied for an exit visa, a process that could take months, and even years, to complete. Complicating matters was the fact that there were penalties awaiting those Russians who asked for permission to leave. One woman who came to the United States during the late twentieth century explained what happened when someone applied for an exit visa:

Soviet Jews protest the Soviet government's strict exit visa requirements. Getting permission to leave the Soviet Union was very difficult.

As a Soviet citizen submits papers requiring a visa, he loses his job. That's not the law, but it's as inevitable as Lenin's portrait in a bureaucrat's office. An odd job may turn up, perhaps in a remote district not caught up with the latest bulletins, but don't count on that. You are reduced to living on savings or loans from friends.[51]

Other recent immigrants from Russia considered unemployment a blessing, because most of their time was spent going from one government office to another making sure that all the correct forms and applications had been filled out, filed, and approved. Even personal possessions needed to be documented to make sure that no citizen was leaving the country with what the Soviet government called valuable "national treasures." To many immigrants, this procedure was especially galling, for it meant that government officials could confiscate anything they wanted under the guise of stopping precious goods from being taken illegally from the country. This measure applied to everything from rare books to family heirlooms. One woman described her experience with Soviet officials when a set of family china was being examined:

I had a lovely set of old china, originally my grandmother's which my mother had given me as a wedding gift. I brought it in so the authorities could take a look at it. The official in charge of the inspection was a particularly unpleasant woman . . . [who]

guessed how much it meant to me. So she went through one book of regulations, then another, then the first, looking for some excuse. Finally she seemed to give up. She took out a big rubber stamp . . . picked up one of my saucers, looked at it carefully—and brought the stamp down so hard that the dish broke into ten pieces.[52]

Once an exit visa was secured and travel arrangements made, the next step was the actual departure from the Soviet Union. For many, this should have been an exciting moment, but according to some, the procedures gave the Soviet bureaucracy a chance to inflict last-minute humiliations. A Russian journalist remembered that when he left Moscow in 1978, he saw families whose belongings were confiscated by government officials just as the immigrants were preparing to board the plane. The reporter's own typewriter was damaged, with several keys broken off, and he recalled that before any of the immigrants could board the plane, government officials:

pawed through every pair of pants, rapped the tops and bottoms of the suitcases and slashed through them with a knife. A customs official took the dresses and underwear of the seven-year-old daughter of my sister and lifting them high over the table, slowly felt through every strap and seam. My sister began to cry. "I can't stand it," she cried. "Pawing and pulling out our underwear in front of everyone. What am I, a criminal?"[53]

years they have gotten used to the fact that it is forbidden to say anything and they have to do as they are told. It is forbidden to refuse. There are no pure human rights.[54]

To non-Russians, this unwillingness to criticize the Soviet Union and its policies proved puzzling. American criticisms of the Soviet Union were commonplace, especially during the cold war period. But to Soviet immigrants, criticisms of their government often translated into criticisms of their homeland, and many took offense. One older Russian immigrant, born during the Russian Revolution, explained this strange loyalty to an interviewer: "Russians know their living standard is very low. They understand that they do not have democracy or freedom of speech. [Yet] they are very proud of being a part of the Great Soviet Empire. . . . It is considered good to be feared by neighbors."[55]

Many recent Russian immigrants faced unemployment, strict exit visa requirements, and invasive searches as they tried to leave.

A Proud People

The more recent Russian immigrants also dealt with the problem of relinquishing their sense of national identity. Doing so caused difficulties for many immigrants, despite the harsh life in the Soviet Union. As one elderly immigrant explained:

It was impossible for me to speak badly of my own country where I had lived all my life. The Russian people are far from bad, but they are an intimidated people. After sixty

From Communism to Capitalism

Life under Soviet rule meant growing up and living in an oppressive regime. This environment affected the way Soviet citizens viewed their government, which was mostly with suspicion and hostility, and this attitude remains one of the few constants

The NYANA

One of the things that most Russian immigrants who came to the United States during the 1970s hoped to put behind them were the bureaucratic headaches that accompanied just about every aspect of Soviet life. Unfortunately, among the first American institutions they encountered was one more reminiscent of the old Soviet-style bureaucracy than of the promised American freedom and efficiency.

The first stop for immigrants arriving in New York City was the New York Agency for New Americans (NYANA), which helped immigrants with loans until they could support themselves. A family of four received approximately $180 a month to be put toward rent, with each family member allotted an additional $100 for monthly expenses. To receive this support, however, the immigrants had to fill out numerous forms and abide by a host of rules. For many immigrants, this process was a disappointing introduction to American life; it also aroused suspicion that their adopted country really did not want them. Their experiences with the NYANA also raised questions about an America where the dollar seemed more important than people and a bureaucracy that, like that of the Soviet Union, seemed mired in inefficiency and unsympathetic to the problems of the people it was supposed to help.

---

among Russian immigrants of all generations. People in the Soviet Union grew up learning that the United States was a terrible enemy and that the American way of life was a source of potential destruction to Russian values. To dismiss these notions when they arrived in the United States was hard. As one Russian immigrant said, "When we ask[ed], Why do we live so badly? We are told [by the Soviet government] that it is because we're encircled by capitalist countries [such as the United States] who are trying to destroy us. From childhood on, we're taught that we are under a constant threat."[56]

The Soviets' attitude toward capitalist America created many problems for new immigrants. For one, Soviet immigrants faced vast political and cultural differences in their new country. One Russian émigré explained that, although he was very appreciative of the freedom America had to offer, coming to the United States meant going to the opposite extreme. "There is too much freedom," he said, "with everyone allowed to live according to purely individual taste. There is simply no consensus about national purpose . . . everything is permitted."[57]

Difficulties often surfaced when the immigrants set out to find work. For former Soviet citizens, the idea of looking for a job was completely unheard of. In the Soviet Union, everyone who was physically able to work was guaranteed employment. No one had to search for work. The idea of applying for a job and competing with other applicants by going through an interview process and preparing a résumé left many Russian immigrants perplexed.

Also confounding were the basic unpleasantries of day-to-day life, some of which the immigrants thought they had left behind. If trying to find a job weren't nerve-wracking enough, the threat of losing a job was also a great source of anxiety. Furthermore, many immigrants found that they still had to deal with unscrupulous landlords, dishonest store owners, and even callous government bureaucrats, all of which they had been used to in the Soviet Union but naively thought they had escaped by coming to America. In addition, many immigrants were reluctant to join political parties or participate in special interest groups, still fearing that they would be persecuted for doing so.

Too Many Choices

Perhaps the most challenging aspect of American life, though, was the sheer number of choices one faced every day. For many Soviet citizens, what they wore or ate or watched on television was determined only by what was available. The idea of being able to acquire almost any sort of goods under any circumstances left many Russians overwhelmed. One Soviet writer described his own reaction the first time he visited an American department store: "Upon seeing the piles of shoes, the heaps

For many Russian immigrants, getting used to the variety of available goods and services is a challenging adjustment.

of clothing . . . besides a multitude of products, goods and items the purpose of which we don't understand—then the Soviet man is simply thunderstruck."[58]

For many Soviet immigrants, the opportunity to buy goods of any kind required a major psychological adjustment. In a country like Russia, and later the Soviet Union, where the government tells its people what they can and cannot have, citizens become passive. Once in America, after becoming used to making choices and using the buying power that was available to them, many Russian immigrants felt that for the first time they had some measure of control over their own lives.

One Vote, One Candidate, One Party

Another area where the Russian immigrants find that they have real choices is at the ballot box, yet historically, they have not utilized that option. Even though many Russian immigrants have lived and raised their families in the United States for years, their influence in American politics has been minimal. There are no known Russian-born politicians. In many major cities, leaders of the Russian community are never heard from, unlike the leaders of other ethnic groups who act as vocal and visible representatives of their respective communities.

Because of their relatively low profile in politics, the Russians have never made the kind of political connections that generate jobs, money, and votes. Some experts believe that the oppressive czarist and Communist regimes under which many Rus-

sians lived has played an important role in the political passivity of Russian immigrants in America. During the period of Communist rule, for instance, all Soviet citizens were required to vote, even though there was little doubt as to the election's outcome. Unlike American elections where there is a choice between candidates and platforms, Soviets voted for a single candidate who ran unopposed. Even after the collapse of the Soviet Union in 1991, Russian elections were still decided more by those who were in power than by the popular ballot.

Increasingly, though, many Russian immigrants are beginning to see that their casting a vote at election time can, in fact, make a difference. And for many Russian immigrants, the simple act of voting reaffirmed for them one of the important reasons for coming to the United States. As one recent immigrant commented after the 2000 presidential elections, "In Russia it didn't matter if you vote or not—the result is the same. Here, when you see the news on TV, you understand that you can change something with your vote."[59] Another immigrant, who taught and studied American democracy, was impressed with the privacy Americans have when voting. When asked outside a polling place whom she voted for, she replied through a translator, "Nyet [No] I'm exercising my American liberty of privacy. In the Soviet Union, I was not able to do that. My whole life I have lived under fear and under the burden of always saying different from what I'm thinking and thinking different from what I was saying."[60]

"Jewish, Not Russian"

Perhaps one of the most troubling problems confronting the latest wave of Russian immigrants concerns the Russian Jews. Growing up in the Soviet Union, these individuals had little or no instruction in Jewish history and culture. They did not worship in synagogues, attend Jewish schools, or observe the customs of the Jewish religion. Even though the Soviet government recognized the distinctions between Jews and non-Jews, stamping passports and official papers as "Jewish" or "Russian," it was primarily for the purpose of singling out the Jewish people for political or legal discrimination.

Upon their arrival in America, these immigrants were not welcomed by other Russian Jews or their descendants, and they were often insulted by the initial treatment they received. Many of the younger immigrant Jews had no idea that an earlier generation of Russian Jews had come to the United States and were shocked to find out that they had established themselves in America for more than a century.

Others belittled the contributions of the earlier generations. Sylvia Rothchild in her book *A Special Legacy: An Oral History of Soviet Jewish Emigrés in the United States* describes one such instance:

> "We are the best immigrants ever to have come to America," said one former [Jewish] member of the Moscow Symphony to one of the Jewish leaders in his community. "We have important contributions to make. We have nothing in common with the illiterate backward *shetl* [village] Jews who came at the turn of the century." He [the former symphony member] was unaware that his contempt for Yiddish-speaking *shetl* Jews would disturb his listener or that most of the affluent university-educated Jews he met were the children or grandchildren of *shetl* Jews.

For many, though, coming to the United States reawakened in them a desire to participate in the Russian Jewish community. Today, many Russian Jews attend synagogue and engage in the cultural traditions of the Jewish religion.

Who Are You?

The variety of choices aside, another problem that many contemporary Russian immigrants face involves both national and cultural identity. Because they have moved to the United States, they no longer consider themselves Russian, but they do not necessarily think of themselves as American either. Caught between the political and ideological identities of two countries that have been at odds for many years many Russian immigrants developed an ambivalence or doubt about who they are.

Although earlier generations saw themselves as Russian Jews, Russians, or Russian refugees, more recent arrivals have grappled with the problem of what to call themselves. The labels are as assorted as Russians themselves: Russian American, Russian American Jew, Soviet American, and Soviet-emigrant Jew. Each label connotes something very specific that, if nothing else, reminds Americans that the Russians are not one people but, instead, a diverse mixture of cultures, traditions, and faiths.

CHAPTER SIX

Strangers No Longer

W hen Mikhail Gorbachev became the Soviet premier in 1985, he took over an empire in desperate need of reform. During the late 1980s, the Soviet Union fell into economic decline, and the power of the government was rapidly disintegrating. Ethnic groups throughout the USSR battled each other for control, and the entire Soviet political system was on the verge of collapse. In this volatile political and economic climate, many Russians sought to leave the country.

Gorbachev made it easier for them to do so. He began by easing the travel restrictions that had formerly prevented Soviet citizens from emigrating at will. At the same time, he loosened emigration controls in an effort to ease domestic tension, an act he hoped would put the Soviet Union on a new path to political and economic stability, and perhaps improve relations with the United States.

Many Soviet citizens took advantage of the new laws, visiting friends and relatives who lived in other parts of the Soviet Union and even those who had left the country years before. Russian Jews, in particular, enjoyed their new freedom of movement. By 1991, just before the collapse of the Soviet Union, more than 250,000 Soviet Jews emigrated. Although the majority settled in Israel, approximately

Mikhail Gorbachev's reforms made it easier for Russians to leave the Soviet Union.

100,000 came to the United States, many making their homes in New York City.

"We Speak English"

This most recent wave of Russian immigrants arrived in a country that was very different from the one to which earlier generations had come. The Russian presence in America during the 1990s was much larger and more visible than it had been a century earlier. The newer immigrants were also more interested in assimilating into the American mainstream than were the earlier generations that came before them. Today, more and more Russians display an eagerness to adopt Western ways and attitudes.

Signs that Russian immigrants have become a part of mainstream American society can be found in cities and towns across the United States. In Cleveland, Ohio, for instance, where it is estimated that approximately forty-three thousand Russian-speaking people now reside, many local businesses have worked hard to build relationships with their Russian customers. This effort has included everything from learning Russian phrases to greet the customers to stocking special foods that Russian immigrant customers use in their cooking. Some businesses translated their store policies into Russian, while others hired Russian immigrants to work for them. One company has even arranged for local cable programming to carry programs in Russia and has published a Russian-language magazine.

This effort to reach out to Russian immigrants has been overwhelmingly successful. In one health food co-op, a Russian immigrant who worked there noticed that a cross-cultural exchange was taking place. "I work at the check-out counter and I see non-Russian people getting some of the herbs and vegetables, which originally were stocked for the Russians," she explained. "But I also suggest to the Russians that they try some new things, which they probably did not have in their own country. Things like soy milk and salad greens have proved to be very popular." Another store owner agreed: "One thing to remember is that forming relationships and building trust can be very important to [Russian immigrants]. They grew up in a regime that often did not work in their favor, so they had to build friendships whenever they did business."[61]

Russian store owners have also tried to reach out to non-Russian customers. In many Russian neighborhoods, more and more Russian-owned businesses display signs that state "We Speak English." These efforts have brought them good rapport with their non-Russian neighbors and have, in turn, broadened their circle of customers.

Living the American Dream

Today, more and more Russian immigrants, like the store owners, are starting their own companies. Although many of the new Russian entrepreneurs started out with little money, their high level of education and expertise in many areas have proven to be invaluable assets in establishing their own businesses. A spokesman for the U.S. Department of Commerce recently stated:

It's mind-boggling how many Ph.D.'s per capita there are [among the new wave of Russian immigrants]. To say that their education level is world-class probably understates things. It gives them a leg up. Many of these people are exceptionally strong in the hard sciences like biology, physics, and chemistry. Many of them are starting software companies and other technology-based businesses. Consulting companies are also very popular.[62]

Some of the current crop of Russian businesses are Boris Lelchitski's Sports International, a scouting agency for women professional basketball players, founded in 1996; Boris Mankovsky's J. E. International Company, which imports Moldovan wine, established in 1997; Norman Peselev's International Education Center in Washington, D.C., which provides tours and seminars for visiting Russian entrepreneurs and executives; and Irina Kouznetsova's IBK

Rova Farms

Built on sixteen hundred acres near Cassville, New Jersey, Rova Farms was founded during the 1930s as a vacation resort by members of various New York and Philadelphia Russian social clubs. The idea behind Rova Farms was to create a relaxing environment where Russian Americans could come and socialize with each other.

At one time, the resort bustled with vacationers. During the 1950s and '60s, Rova Farms reached its peak, offering a variety of sports, activities, and dining to Russian immigrants. But as its original members died and their children became more assimilated into American society, fewer had reason to patronize the resort. Today, Rova Farms is situated on a much smaller piece of land with only a restaurant and bar. Yet it maintains a busy schedule, hosting various religious and social events throughout the year.

Corporation, which exports building materials to Russia and Ukraine.

Many of these businesses capitalize on using Russian goods and labor that are cheaper than American labor and products. Some of the new businesses also rely on software programs written in Russian. These programs save money because they save time; workers can read them in their native language rather than having to learn English first. Such developments present a very attractive alternative to both American and Russian businessmen looking for good workers and good products that are, at the same time, cost effective.

Problems Emigrate Too

Although the Russian immigrant experience in the United States has been positive overall and many of the recent immigrants have worked hard to fit in to American society, in recent years there has been increased attention in the media to one unpleasant but profitable aspect of Russian immigration: organized crime. Although law enforcement officials are unsure how extensive Russian organized crime is in the United States, the fact is that organized criminal activity does exist and it is historically linked to Russian immigration.

Crime among the Russian immigrant population is nothing new. Since the arrival of the first Russian immigrants during the nineteenth century, there have been criminals and criminal activity. Russian neighborhoods were plagued by robberies and murders. Furthermore, gambling and loan-sharking activities and paying "protection money" to ensure that businesses were not terrorized by local thieves and thugs were common occurrences.

"Little Odessa"

During the 1970s, the small waterfront community of Brighton Beach, Brooklyn, was falling into a state of disrepair. A dramatic influx of Russian immigrants during that decade, however, quickly energized the town. Connected to the rest of New York City by four subway lines, Brighton Beach remains the heart of Russian American culture not only in New York but in the rest of the country as well.

The area is often referred to as "Little Odessa," a reference to the popular sea resort city of Odessa in southern Russia, and in many ways the neighborhood came to resemble the old Russian and Soviet empires. Residents from Russia, Ukraine, Georgia, Uzbekistan, and other former Soviet states live side by side. Many of the stores have Russian signs, and the streets are filled with the sounds of people speaking Russian. Visitors to the neighborhood can taste and smell the Russian presence, for the bakeries, coffee shops, and restaurants on every block serve the "native" foods of their homeland, including borscht (beetroot soup) and black bread.

Beginning in the 1970s, however, the nature and scope of these enterprises changed. In 1975, the American government began to put increased pressure on the Soviet government to allow Soviet Jews, including those who had been imprisoned as political prisoners and dissidents, to immigrate to Israel. Part of this pressure came in the form of a threat by the American government that if the Jews were not allowed to leave, the Soviet Union would lose its Most Favored Nation (MFN) status, a reciprocal trading status that provides a country with the lowest available taxes on its exports to the United States. Such a sanction would have crippled the Soviet economy.

In response to the U.S. request, the head of the Soviet KGB decided that if the Americans wanted the emigration of Soviet Jews, he would permit it. In addition, though, the Communist government decided that it would also free other Russians, many of them hardened criminals who were imprisoned in jails and gulags, or prison camps. Thus arrived in the United States the first massive influx of Soviet criminals, numbering about forty-five thousand.

Many of these new arrivals settled in Brighton Beach, Brooklyn, which became one of the largest Russian communities in the country. It was also here that the Russian Mafia established its headquarters. Over the course of the next fifteen years, Russian criminals expanded their activities from a neighborhood extortion racket to a multibillion-dollar international crime cartel involved in everything from gasoline-distribution scams and drug running to prostitution, stock market fraud, and money laundering. After the collapse of the Communist government in 1991, the Russian Mafia continued to grow as more Russian criminals escaped to the United States.

The sharp increase in Russian organized crime hurt the Russian immigrant community in the United States. The image of the Russian gangster has contributed to a stereotype that all Russian immigrants are corrupt, violent criminals who are not interested in making an honest living. Although many Russian immigrants agree that there is a crime problem, they also believe that the American press has exaggerated its size and influence, and in the process tarnished the reputations of honest immigrants who have worked hard to succeed in the United States.

Difficulty Assimilating

Despite the problem of organized crime, Russian immigrants have managed to battle negative images of their people and culture. By holding on to many of their traditions, learning English, and embracing the opportunities America offers, many of them have overcome countless obstacles to assimilation. However, some concerns remain. For many Russian immigrants, a number of changes have begun to occur within their neighborhoods. As thriving and bustling as many Russian immigrant communities are, the populations there have decreased over time. As more and more Russian immigrants become accustomed to American ways, many have decided to forgo the security of the Russian community. For some, this means relocating to

A Homecoming

On August 18, 1997, in the small town of Voskresensk, Russia, located sixty miles from Moscow, a crowd anxiously gathered. Soon to arrive were three Russian players from an American hockey team, the Detroit Red Wings, two of whom had been born and raised in Voskresensk. This was more than a homecoming, however, for the players had brought with them the Stanley Cup, the prize awarded to the champion of the National Hockey League (NHL).

When the members of the team and the cup arrived, an emotional crowd greeted them. Igor Larionov and Slava Kozlov, the two players who grew up in Voskresensk and learned to play hockey there, took the opportunity to thank the town for supporting them throughout their careers, even though they now played for an American team thousands of miles away.

These Russians and many others playing in the NHL have not forgotten their origins. They work to raise funds to support the revitalization of hockey in Russia. As part of that effort, Red Wings

players also took the Stanley Cup to Moscow, where they posed for photographs and signed autographs not far from the Lenin Mausoleum in the city's Red Square.

Igor Larionov is one of many Russians who currently play in the NHL.

neighborhoods where not everyone is Russian. For others, it means leaving behind certain cultural traditions such as the Russian Orthodox Church, Russian food and history, or the Russian language.

Forgoing that security also means facing the fact that the promise of America was not

all the immigrants had hoped it would be. Even though many Russians agree that living in a democracy is preferable to living under Communist rule, they also realize that living in the United States does not always guarantee political or economic freedom. Some immigrants upon their arrival in

America were taken aback by the shocking social conditions in American cities. As one immigrant described the first time he and his wife saw a Russian neighborhood in New York City, "We were horrified by the broken houses and the filth."[63] Others were surprised at the often impersonal relations between Americans and the residents' inability or unwillingness to get to know each other.

Situations like these isolated some immigrants, making them feel that they did not fit in to American society very well. One Russian immigrant, who was able to find a well-paying job as an engineer not long after his arrival in America, explained, "I was very happy the first two years. I thought I was adjusted and had no problems. Now, after four years, I see that I am not. The longer I stay, the more I see that it will take years. If you change your country you can never really belong, never really be happy."[64]

Young Immigrants: Fitting In

Nowhere is the struggle more obvious than with young immigrants, particularly teenagers. No matter where they live, teenagers often struggle to fit in with their peers. For immigrant teens, the desire to fit in is even more pronounced because, as one Russian immigrant teenager explained, "Émigrés in American schools are often taunted by their classmates, who call them communists, and yet many of them emigrated before they could fully understand what it meant to be Russian, let alone communist."[65]

On the surface, many teenage immigrants are doing well. They live in the cities and towns of America, go to American

A challenge for many young Russian Americans is finding acceptance among their American peers.

schools, and listen to American rock and roll. Such evidence is superficial, however. For young Russian immigrants and the children of immigrants, the real challenge is feeling comfortable with being both a Russian and an American. It is a challenge many have trouble expressing to friends and family. Says one teenage immigrant:

> I miss my friends in Russia very much. Except for my brother I have nobody like them to talk to here. I just don't know what to talk about with Americans. The cultures are so different. . . . I have some American friends. . . . They were interested in understanding Russia. Russia is strange even for Russians. You can't understand it in your mind. It is an emotional experience.[66]

And, yet, despite the emotional struggle, immigrant teenagers, in fact Russian immigrants in general, contend that the challenge of finding their place in American society is just part of their overall experience—an experience in which things are not all wonderful or all terrible. Instead, it is a blending of both. For even though the latest wave of immigrants to the United States in many ways came better prepared for life in a new country, they still face many of the same problems upon arrival that earlier generations of Russian immigrants did. Furthermore, many immigrants have found greater freedom to work and live as they please, but the freedom has come at a price, as some immigrants worry about losing touch with their history and their culture. In spite of these concerns, though, Russian immigrants continue to come to the United States, a fact that illustrates their courage and determination to become part of America's diverse population. As one young immigrant explained, "I love being a Russian-American, though I feel more Russian in my heart. I can keep my Russian culture and at the same time try to absorb the best of the U.S."[67]

NOTES

Chapter 1: Strangers in Their Homeland

1. Quoted in Abba Eban, *Heritage: Civilization and the Jews.* New York: Summit Books, 1984, p. 239.
2. Quoted in Zivi Gitelman, *A Century of Ambivalence: The Jews of Russia and the Soviet Union, 1881 to the Present.* New York: Schocken Books, 1988, p. 7.
3. Quoted in Ronald Sanders, *Shores of Refuge: A Hundred Years of Jewish Immigration.* New York: Henry Holt, 1988, p. 3.
4. Quoted in Sanders, *Shores of Refuge,* p 4.
5. Quoted in Edward Crankshaw, *The Shadow of the Winter Palace: Russia's Drift to Revolution, 1825–1917.* New York: Viking Press, 1976, p. 282.
6. Quoted in Sanders, *Shores of Refuge,* p. 13.
7. Quoted in Sanders, *Shores of Refuge,* p. 14.
8. Quoted in Milton Meltzer, *The Jewish Americans: A History in Their Own Words, 1650–1950.* New York: Thomas Y. Crowell, 1982, p. 66.

Chapter 2: Coming to America

9. Quoted in Sanders, *Shores of Refuge,* p. 25.
10. Quoted in Dorothy and Thomas Hoobler, *The Jewish American Family Album.* New York: Oxford University Press, 1995, p. 30.
11. Quoted in Sanders, *Shores of Refuge,* p. 58.
12. Quoted in Sanders, *Shores of Refuge,* p. 60.
13. Quoted in Sanders, *Shores of Refuge,* p. 58.
14. Quoted in Hoobler, *The Jewish American Family Album,* p. 28.
15. Quoted in Hoobler, *The Jewish American Family Album,* p. 31.
16. Quoted in Sanders, *Shores of Refuge,* p. 66.
17. Quoted in Ann Novotny, *Strangers at the Door: Ellis Island, Castle Garden, and the Great Migration to America.* Riverside, CT: Chatham Press, 1971, p. 50.
18. Quoted in Sanders, *Shores of Refuge,* p. 66.
19. Quoted in Sanders, *Shores of Refuge,* p. 67.
20. Quoted in Sanders, *Shores of Refuge,* p. 68.
21. Quoted in Sanders, *Shores of Refuge,* p. 70.
22. Quoted in Sanders, *Shores of Refuge,* p. 70.
23. Quoted in Sanders, *Shores of Refuge,* p. 67.
24. Quoted in Sanders, *Shores of Refuge,* p. 72.
25. Quoted in Virginia Yans-McLaughlin and Marjorie Lightman, with the Statue of Liberty–Ellis Island Foundation, *Ellis Island and the Peopling of America: The Official Guide.* New York: New Press, 1990, p. 143.

Chapter 3: The Three Waves of Russian Immigration

26. Quoted in W. Bruce Lincoln, *Red Victory: A History of the Russian Civil War.* New York: Touchstone Books, 1989, p. 32.
27. Quoted in Lincoln, *Red Victory,* p. 32.
28. Quoted in Modern History Sourcebook. "Abdication of Nikolai II, March 15, 1917." www.dur.ac.uk/~dml0www/abdicatn.html.
29. Quoted in Victor Ripp, *Moscow to Main Street: Among the Russian Emigrés.* Boston: Little, Brown, 1984, p. 21.
30. Quoted in Sylvia Rothchild, *A Special Legacy: An Oral History of Soviet Jewish Emigrés in the United States.* New York: Simon and Schuster, 1985, p. 243.
31. Quoted in Rothchild, *A Special Legacy,* p. 114.
32. Quoted in Gitelman, *A Century of Ambivalence,* p. 270.
33. Quoted in Avi Lewis, "Remembering Dancer Mikhail Baryshnikov's Great Defection," May 17, 1999. www.infoculture.cbc.ca/archives/dance/dance_05171999_defection.html.

Chapter 4: Becoming American

34. Quoted in Hoobler, *The Jewish American Family Album,* p. 59.
35. Quoted in Hoobler, *The Jewish American Family Album,* p. 56.
36. Quoted in Jerome Davis, *The Russian Immigrant.* New York: Arno Press, 1969, p. 35.
37. Quoted in Davis, *The Russian Immigrant,* p. 35.
38. Quoted in Davis, *The Russian Immigrant,* p. 25.
39. Quoted in Davis, *The Russian Immigrant,* p. 25.
40. Quoted in Hoobler, *The Jewish American Family Album,* p. 53.
41. Quoted in Davis, *The Russian Immigrant,* p. 41.
42. Quoted in Hoobler, *The Jewish American Family Album,* p. 83.
43. Quoted in Davis, *The Russian Immigrant,* p. 61.
44. Quoted in Hoobler, *The Jewish American Family Album,* p. 46.
45. Quoted in Hoobler, *The Jewish American Family Album,* p. 46.
46. Quoted in Peter Morton Caan, *Ellis Island Interviews: In Their Own Words.* New York: Facts On File, 1997, p. 259.
47. Quoted in Hoobler, *The Jewish American Family Album,* p. 92.
48. Quoted in Hoobler, *The Jewish American Family Album,* p. 76.

Chapter 5: Differences Within and Without

49. Quoted in Novotny, *Strangers at the Door,* p. 123.
50. Quoted in Novotny, *Strangers at the Door,* p. 124.
51. Quoted in Ripp, *Moscow to Main Street,* p. 39.
52. Quoted in Ripp, *Moscow to Main Street,* pp. 39–40.
53. Quoted in Ripp, *Moscow to Main Street,* p. 42.
54. Quoted in Rothchild, *A Special Legacy,* p. 260.
55. Quoted in Rothchild, *A Special Legacy,* p. 116.
56. Quoted in Rothchild, *A Special Legacy,* p. 117.
57. Quoted in Ripp, *Moscow to Main Street,* p. 129.

58. Quoted in Ripp, *Moscow to Main Street*, p. 228.

59. Quoted in Associated Press Online, "Recount—Former Soviets," November 11, 2001, http://ehostvgw19.epnet.com/ehost.asp?key=204.179.122.141_8000_1358992231

60. Quoted in Associated Press Online, "Recount—Former Soviets."

Chapter 6: Strangers No Longer

61. Quoted in Harriet Tramer, "Businesses Cultivating Russian Relationships," *Crain's Cleveland Business,* October 16, 2000, p. 21.

62. Quoted in *Inc.,* "Immigrants Viewed as 'World-Class,'" July 1999, p. 22.

63. Quoted in Rothchild, *A Special Legacy,* p. 304.

64. Quoted in Rothchild, *A Special Legacy,* p. 301.

65. Quoted in Ripp, *Moscow to Main Street*, p. 114.

66. Tatyana Zamenova, *In Their Own Voices: Teenage Refugees from Russia Speak Out.* New York: Rosen, 1995, p. 33.

67. Quoted in Zamenova, *In Their Own Voices,* pp. 44–45.

FOR FURTHER READING

Books

Dorothy and Thomas Hoobler, *The Jewish American Family Album*. New York: Oxford University Press, 1995. An overview of the history of Jewish Americans told almost entirely in first-person accounts.

Paul Magocsi, *The Russian Americans*. New York: Chelsea House, 1989. A history of Russian immigrants in the United States.

Milton Meltzer, *The Jewish Americans: A History in Their Own Words, 1650–1950*. New York: Thomas Y. Crowell, 1982. Using first-person accounts, Meltzer looks at the impact of the Jewish Americans in the United States.

R. Conrad Stein, *Ellis Island*. Chicago: Childrens Press, 1992. A brief history of Ellis Island.

Tatyana Zamenova, *In Their Own Voices: Teenage Refugees from Russia Speak Out*. New York: Rosen, 1995. Six refugees from varying backgrounds talk about their lives in the Soviet Union and in America.

Internet Sources

Associated Press Online, "Recount—Former Soviets," November 16, 2000. http://ehostvgw19.epnet.com/ehost.asp?key=204.1 79.122.141_8000_1358992231.

History Channel, "Discusses Defection to the West," interview with Svetlana Alliluyeva. www.historychannel.com/cgi-bin/frameit. cgi?p=http%3A//www.historychannel.com/ speeches/archive/speech_6.html.

J. Kniesmeyer and D. Brecher, "Beyond the Pale: The History of the Jews in Russia." www.friends-partners.org/partners/beyond-the-pale/index.html, 1995.

Avi Lewis, "Remembering Dancer Mikhail Baryshnikov's Great Defection," May 17, 1999. www.infoculture.cbc.ca/ archives/dance/dance_05171999_defection. html.

Library of Congress, "In the Beginning There Was the Word: The Russian Church and Native Alaskan Cultures." www.loc.gov/ exhibits/russian/sla.html.

Modern History Sourcebook, "Abdication of Nikolai II, March 15, 1917." www.dur.ac.uk/~dm10www/abdicatn.html.

———, "Mary Antin: A Little Jewish Girl in the Russian Pale," 1890. www.fordham. edu/halsall/mod/1890antin.html.

James Harvey Robinson and Charles Beard, eds., *Readings in Modern European History,* vol. 2. 1908. www.shsu.edu/~his_ ncp/Assass.html.

WORKS CONSULTED

Books

David M. Brownstone, Douglass Brownstone, and Irene M. Franck, *Island of Hope, Island of Tears: Through Ellis Island to the New World,* New York: Barnes & Noble Books, 2000. A collection of oral histories detailing the immigrant experience at Ellis Island.

Peter Morton Caan, *Ellis Island Interviews: In Their Own Words.* New York: Facts On File, 1997. A collection of interviews with immigrants from all over the world about coming to America and their experiences.

Edward Crankshaw, *The Shadow of the Winter Palace: Russia's Drift to Revolution, 1825–1917.* New York: Viking Press, 1976. A history of the events leading up to the Bolshevik revolution.

Roger Daniels, *Coming to America: A History of Immigration and Ethnicity in American Life.* New York: HarperCollins, 1990. A broad overview chronicling the history of American immigration.

Jerome Davis, *The Russian Immigrant.* New York: Arno Press, 1969. A reprint of an early sociological study done by the author on the Russian immigrant.

Abba Eban, *Heritage: Civilization and the Jews.* New York: Summit Books, 1984. A general history of the Jewish people.

James O. Finckenauer and Elin J. Waring, *Russian Mafia in America: Immigration, Culture, and Crime.* Boston: Northeastern University Press, 1998. A history of the Russian Mafia, exploring its causes and impact in American society.

Gerald Freeze, ed., *Russia: A History.* New York: Oxford University Press, 1997. A general history of Russia with an emphasis on the modern period.

Zivi Gitelman, *A Century of Ambivalence: The Jews of Russia and the Soviet Union, 1881 to the Present.* New York: Schocken Books, 1988. A historical look at the history of the Jewish people in Russia.

Robert A. Karlowich, *We Fall and Rise: Russian-Language Newspapers in New York City, 1889–1914.* Metuchen, NJ: Scarecrow Press, 1991. An interesting exploration of the role of the Russian-language newspapers within Russian immigrant culture and in American society as a whole.

W. Bruce Lincoln, *Red Victory: A History of the Russian Civil War.* New York: Touchstone Books, 1989. An intensive overview of the people, events, and impact of the Russian civil war.

Fran Markowitz, *A Community in Spite of Itself: Soviet Jewish Emigrés in New York.* Washington, DC: Smithsonian Institution Press, 1993. A study of the Soviet Jewish immigrants who came to the United States during the second and third waves of immigration.

Ann Novotny, *Strangers at the Door: Ellis Island, Castle Garden, and the Great Migration to America.* Riverside, CT: Chatham Press, 1971. A good history of Ellis Island with numerous firsthand accounts.

Victor Ripp, *Moscow to Main Street: Among the Russian Emigrés.* Boston: Little, Brown, 1984. An interesting and entertaining look at how Russian immigrants feel about their homeland and living in the United States.

Sylvia Rothchild, *A Special Legacy: An Oral History of Soviet Jewish Emigrés in the United States.* New York: Simon and Schuster, 1985. A thoughtful and moving account of the lives of several Soviet immigrants.

Ronald Sanders, *Shores of Refuge: A Hundred Years of Jewish Immigration.* New York: Henry Holt, 1988. A sweeping overview of the history of Jewish immigration, focusing on Russian Jews.

Virginia Yans-McLaughlin and Marjorie Lightman, with the Statue of Liberty–Ellis Island Foundation, *Ellis Island and the Peopling of America: The Official Guide.* New York: New Press, 1990. A history and resource guide of Ellis Island.

Periodicals

Robert B. Cullen, with Susan Agrest, Anne Underwood, and Don Shirley, "Emigres: Born in the U.S.S.R.," *Newsweek,* August 19, 1985.

Lynn Ducey, "Russian Resort Fits into the Melting Pot," *Asbury Park Press,* April 20, 2000.

Jennifer Gould, "Energy Aplenty in 'Little Odessa,'" *Village Voice,* March 18, 1997.

Inc., "Immigrants Viewed as 'World-Class,'" July 1999.

Harriet Tramer, "Businesses Cultivating Russian Relationships," *Crain's Cleveland Business,* October 16, 2000.

Bob Wojnowski, "Tears Flow as Cup Comes to Russia's Hockeytown," *Detroit News,* August 20, 1997.

INDEX

PICTURE CREDITS

Cover Photo: Associated Press/AP
Archive Photos, 12, 13, 18, 19, 33, 39, 44, 45, 46, 59, 63,
    66, 69
Associated Press, 92
© Bettman/Corbis, 49, 61, 67, 79
Corbis, 25
Bernard Gotfryd/Archive Photos, 52, 55
© David Hanover/Corbis, 83
Library of Congress, 35, 37, 40, 48
Museum of the City of New York/Archive, 64
Nordik Pressefoto/Archive Photos, 56
Northwind Picture Archives, 16, 17, 22, 24, 30
© Richard T. Nowitz/Corbis, 93
Popperfoto/Archive Photos, 88
© Moshe Shai/Corbis, 81
© Stock Montage, 75, 76

About the Author

Meg Greene Malvasi is a writer and historian who has earned degrees in history and historic preservation. She is the author of ten books, one of which, *Slave Young, Slave Long,* was recognized as a 1999 Honor Book from the Society of School Librarians International for Grades 7 to 12. She is also a regular contributor to *Cobblestone Magazine* and a contributing editor to "History for Children" for *Suite 101.com.* Ms. Greene Malvasi makes her home in Virginia.

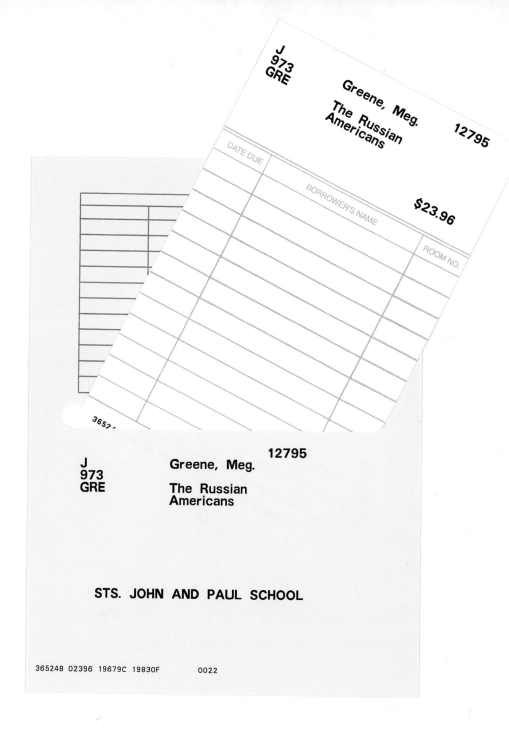

J
973
GRE

Greene, Meg.

The Russian
Americans

12795

$23.96

DATE DUE

BORROWER'S NAME

ROOM NO.

3652

12795

J
973
GRE

Greene, Meg.

The Russian
Americans

STS. JOHN AND PAUL SCHOOL

365248 02396 19679C 19830F   0022